W9-BNX-992

4.95

THE MODERN NATIONS IN

HISTORICAL PERSPECTIVE

ROBIN W. WINKS, *General Editor*

The volumes in this series deal with individual nations or groups of closely related nations, summarizing the chief historical trends and influences that have contributed to each nation's present-day character, problems, and behavior. Recent data are incorporated with established historical background to achieve a fresh synthesis and original interpretation.

The author of this volume, RICHARD M. BRACE, writes from long personal experience in the Maghrib. Graduate of the University of California at Berkeley, he studied in France for nine years and in North Africa for three. He is the author of *The Making of the Modern World* and (with his wife as co-author) *Ordeal in Algeria*. During 1964-65, Dr. Brace takes leave from his position as Professor of Modern History at Northwestern University to study in Algeria under a Rockefeller Foundation grant.

FORTHCOMING VOLUMES IN THE AFRICAN SUBSERIES

British East Africa *by Colin T. Leys*
Central Africa *by Prosser Gifford*
The Congo *by Harry R. Rudin*
Egypt and the Sudan *by Robert Tignor and Robert Collins*
The Horn: Ethiopia, Eritrea, and the Somalilands *by William H. Lewis*
Former French West Africa *by John D. Hargreaves*
Ghana and Nigeria *by John Flint*
Portuguese Africa *by Ronald Chilcote*
Sierra Leone and Liberia *by Christopher Fyfe*

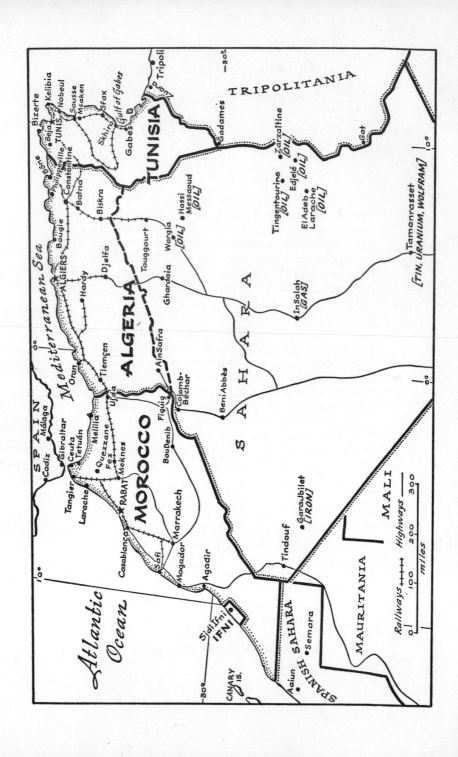

MOROCCO ◆ ALGERIA ◆ TUNISIA ◆

RICHARD M. BRACE

A SPECTRUM BOOK

Prentice-Hall, Inc.

Englewood Cliffs, New Jersey

WINGATE COLLEGE LIBRARY
WINGATE, N. C.

For George Blanksten and Moody Prior

Current printing (last digit):
12 11 10 9 8 7 6 5 4 3

Copyright © 1964 by PRENTICE-HALL, INC., *Engle-wood Cliffs, N.J.* All rights reserved. No part of this book may be reproduced in any form, by mimeograph or any other means, without permission in writing from the publishers. *Library of Congress Catalog Card Number:* 64-23571. Printed in the United States of America —C. P 60105, C 60106

Since the close of the Second World War it is no longer possible for those of the western world to look upon people and nations of other continents as interesting, exotic flora or fauna whose flourishing or fading depend upon a colonialist will or whim. Just as the Latin Americans are no longer safely "our" people, neither are the vastly complicated, infinitely old countries of the Mediterranean basin any longer places where we can comfortably go to make "diggings" into past layers of history. For in these countries history itself is in the saddle, and we must be fortunate to go along on the ride.

The Maghrib is, for example, a significant and participating sector of a worldwide decolonization movement; many countries in Africa, Asia, and Latin America have recently forced the old colonial structures to give ground. Indigenous peoples of these continents have fought both bloody and philosophical battles to move into positions of greater responsibility, to become political leaders in their own area, even to become human beings.

It is also interesting to note that these people of the "third world" (named by the French with infinite *finesse*) are consummately aware of similar struggles of underdeveloped states both near and far. For example, after the "Bay of Pigs" fiasco, the May 12, 1961 issue of *El Moudjahid*, official organ of the nationalist Algerian Liberation Front, carried the headline, "Algeria, Angola, Cuba: the Same Battle."

Battle for what? Not simply for political independence but for individual status and an attempt to extricate North Africa from the economic and social thrust of Western imperialism. That the old imperial structures yielded before the pressures of the various nationalisms is amply demonstrated by a comparison of the world maps of 1945 with those of two decades later. That Soviet imperialism did not yield an inch is equally demonstrable. This evolution of the peoples of the former colonialist areas resulted only in part from the activity of the nationalist forces. The climate of international opinion was remarkably cooperative.

v

40613

The United States and the Soviet Union, the only surviving great powers, favored national self-determination as a matter of policy—if not always in deeds or from similar motivation. And the European colonial powers in the immediate post-1945 world diverted their energies to domestic reconstruction. Thus, the route to independence for the world's peoples was remarkably clear.

Yet French vitality was not so sapped as to agree to this evolution without an eight-year struggle in Indo-China and another of almost similar duration in Algeria. By comparison the protectorates over Morocco and Tunisia were withdrawn in relative peace. The story of these revolutionary and evolutionary developments concerns us not only as history, but also as a determinant in the future Maghrib. These new states, so long slumbering under the imprint of past cultures and tribal ways, yet always on the sensitive edge of western civilization, now face full responsibility for their future.

Living as we do in a shrinking world, they have become our neighbors. Proud of their varied past, a heritage of Greek, Roman, Norman, Ottoman Turk, and above all Arab, they took steps in our direction during the period of French domination. Now they have a difficult choice to make. Without denying the complexities of their past and the positive factors of Arab culture, they must look outward into the modern world for experience, example, and advice if they are to survive in the twentieth century.

No longer do they have colonial scapegoats. They must "do it themselves" or else. They must build new bridges into the world of the present, choose new partners, make new alliances or continue to have faith in the old ones under renewed conditions. Only time can tell how they meet the challenge: whether or not they will write a heroic chapter in their long and rich history.

R. B.

CONTENTS

The independent states we know today as Morocco, Algeria, and Tunisia occupy the lion's share of what medieval Arab geographers called *Geziret-el-Maghrib*, "the island of the west." How could such learned men adopt a name which violated observable conditions? These scholars considered that land could be isolated by elements other than water. The Maghrib, bounded by the Mediterranean in the north, the Sahara in the south, the Atlantic on the west and by three hundred miles of desert running to the Mediterranean between Tripolitania and Cyrenaica, is a land island, isolated from the Nile valley except for the caravan coastal route connecting Gabes with Alexandria.

Geographical Influences

Isolation and compartmentalization characterize the history of this northwestern strip of Africa. The Maghrib resembles Chile in shape, but it stretches east and west instead of north and south. Access to this land mass between the Gulf of Cabes and Tangier from any direction save the Mediterranean side is barred by a formidable series of mountains. These barriers generally follow a northeast/southwest line beginning in lower Morocco with the Atlas (altitude 12,000 feet) and reaching the Aurès system in eastern Tunisia (4,500 feet). These mountains, filled with steep valleys and narrow gorges, denied permanent occupation and control to all invaders.

1

Yet, in our times, these barriers fail to provide solid natural borders between the newly independent states of Morocco, Algeria, and Tunisia, because the orientation of the mountains is east-west while the frontier lines approach a north-south axis. Thus the Moroccan-Algerian southern border (the Colomb-Béchar area) on the Sahara is extremely unstable, and Tunisian claims on Algeria's southeast continue active.

These natural obstacles to the centralized state help to explain the failure of the Moroccan kingdom to control the Berber tribesmen of the Atlas. They also provide us an insight into the independent and recalcitrant posture of the Kabylia Berbers and the Berber tribes of the Aurès toward the regime of President Ahmed Ben Bella.

Mountains and highlands cover roughly one-fourth of the total area of modern Morocco, Algeria, and Tunisia. They form a rather formidable and continuous barrier inside the Mediterranean coastal area at various depths from the coastline, usually about fifty miles inland. Large flatlands can be found in each country. In Morocco the Atlantic plain extends from Tangier to Mogador, and a fine mesa connects Settat with Kenifra. The valley of Moulouya and the eastern steppe provide a large unindented zone. Algeria, the middle state of the former French North African complex, possesses low plains surrounding the cities of Oran and Mostaganem, while the Chélif valley runs parallel to the coast toward Orléansville, sometimes reaching a depth of one hundred miles. In the Algiers region the lush plain of the Mitidja, the showplace of the large French plantations before the Algerian independence of July 1962, long stood as the richest, highest-yielding land in the state. In eastern Algeria, from Philippeville, stretching through Bône beyond the Tunisian border, another lowland area prevents the mountains from isolating the sea. The Tunisian steppe from Hammamet to Gabes, the Medjerda valley, and the Mateur plain provide that country with a proportionally greater lowland area than either of its neighboring states.

The most important, yet little known and virginal natural resource storehouse affecting Algeria, and to a smaller degree Morocco, Tunisia, and Mali, is the upper Sahara. Here, geologists found large resources of natural gas and petroleum in 1956. Before these discoveries, water (or the lack of it) determined the life of the Sahara's peoples.

Should this shortage be overcome and a suspected water table below the desert be found, or should Algerian lowland areas such as the vast plain extending southward from Biskra to the Grand Eastern Erg be developed, the agricultural potential of the country would be powerfully increased. Since discoveries of 1956, attention has usually centered upon the mineral potential of the Sahara. The Maghribi hope the Sahara will not only provide the essential raw materials for an industrial economy, but also a source of energy.

Precisely how the Sahara will influence the economic and political future of Africa is an open question. Its people are almost entirely Arabic- or Berber-speaking and their institutions usually came from the north which may indicate future political and cultural orientation. These traditional forces surely will be submitted to forceful technological change. At the political level it is reasonably certain that of all the chapters in the Evian accords reached by the Provisional Government of the Algerian Republic and the French in March 1961, those governing the Sahara are the most sensitive—the most likely to precipitate difficult political problems if unilaterally disturbed in the next decade. At another level, that of a future unified or federated Africa, the Sahara is seen by some prophets as an amalgam and a source of economic power which should benefit the entire continent and its people. Considerable recent evidence stands between this pleasant dream and its early realization. Those states which border the Sahara have not yet agreed on how to share its wealth, nor are they yet capable of exploiting it themselves.

Reinforcing the isolation and compartmentalization of the inhabitants of the Maghrib is the absence of navigable rivers. In all of Morocco, Algeria, and Tunisia, one river, the Sebu, originating in the Atlas and flowing to Kenitra (former Port Lyautey) can be called a transportation aid. This leaves the Mediterranean coastal entries as the sole link to waterways, which in turn depend upon hospitable ports. These, with the exception of Casablanca on the Atlantic, and Algiers, are hard to find. Basins such as Oran, Philippeville, and Bône help Algeria, and the port of Tunis is adequate to care for most ships. Railroad lines built by the French connect these countries; and an excellent road system, at least along the coastal zone, is another legacy from France. But for quick, dependable, and comfortable transportation the airplane is king in Northwest Africa. Inland surface transportation (that is, north-south movement away from the coastal zone) resembles the time-honored caravans which plied their routes in both directions.

Rainfall, an important conditioner of ways of life, varies greatly in Northwest Africa. It is largely determined by the location of the mountains and the prevailing winds. Thus, along the coast from Cape Bon to Tangier, twenty to forty inches of rain are dropped annually out of the Mediterranean winds. Eastern Morocco benefits from the fact that the Atlantic winds must travel far inland before they reach the Atlas, but rainfall tapers off abruptly at the approaches to the Sahara. A thin east-west strip above that desert receives ten to twenty inches per year and then rapidly, as the southern course is pursued, rainfall declines to less than five inches in any year.

The Maghrib, which until recently was largely under the French tricolor, suffered some isolation from the vibrant Mediterranean culture. This isolation was even more pronounced from sub-Saharan Africa—what the French call *Afrique Noire*—because of the impenetrable desert. Traditionally, too, great disparity of land surface produced a land cut up in many pieces: North Africa suffered from *morcellement*. This then was a land which, by European standards, found that "life, whether it was vegetable, animal, or human was extremely insecure." [1]

An Expanding Population

Probably life was no more insecure in Northwest Africa than in any other part of the developing world. In recent times a striking population increase among Muslims indicates that more children lived and grew to maturity in the area, that the life-span lengthened, and that life was less precarious. When it became available, the French brought penicillin to Africa, and the Maghrib had no serious epidemics or famines after 1942 and 1945. Though it was quite true that food supply also increased, it did not do so as rapidly as population. Take, for example, the changing relationship between population and food supply in Algeria, an area which supported perhaps 2 million inhabitants

---

[1] Roger Le Tourneau, *Évolution politique de l'Afrique du Nord musulmane 1920-1960* (Paris: Colin, 1962), p. 13.

in 1830 at the moment of the French invasion of Algiers. In 1900, and again by 1930, the population had doubled. By 1980 it is expected to reach 20 million. Yet it is also a startling fact that the annual per capita consumption of wheat by the Muslim inhabitant of Algeria dropped from four quintals* in 1900 to two and one-half in 1940, and to two in 1950.

Because the most recent census figures were collected at different times in Morocco, Algeria, and Tunisia, the results are far from accurate. The total population reaches approximately 28,000,000— 12,000,000 of whom live in Morocco. Perhaps an equal number inhabit independent Algeria (including the Algerian Sahara), and 4,000,000 live in Tunisia.

Sharp changes characterize recent population patterns in these three countries. The most important has already been mentioned: the rapid growth of the Muslim majority in the last half century. The significance of this increase heightens when examined against the exodus of Europeans since 1956, when Morocco and Tunisia became independent, and, in the case of Algeria, since March 1962, when the Evian accords were signed. In 1954, some 1,770,000 Europeans inhabited the area. In 1963 there were perhaps 540,000 left. The most casual study of the recent history of these three countries explains this change. The basic point to be made here is that European influence, like European numbers, has sharply declined in the last decade. Independence and Arabization replaced Euro-colonial institutions, for better say the nationalists, and for worse say the Europeans—particularly the colonials who left.

EUROPEANS IN NORTHWEST AFRICA

	1954	1964 (estimate)
Algeria	910,000	100,000
Morocco	615,000	300,000
Tunisia	245,000	140,000
Total	1,770,000	540,000

In the North African Muslim mind, the Europeans are the people who came and developed the land in the nineteenth century largely

* One quintal equals 100 kgs. or 220.46 lbs.

for themselves. Europeans disembarked, squatted on indigenous land, or took it by force of arms, and built it up. Although some have remained under the new independent regimes, the ground rules have been changed. Since the new rules are less favorable to Europeans and the independence movement was accompanied by violence, the immediate future relationship between European and Muslim is not particularly close. Yet the new states require European technicians and teachers to maintain their existing industrial complex and to develop additional agricultural and industrial production.

Most of the Europeans adopted French citizenship, which was made easily accessible to the large members of Spanish, Italian, Maltese, and other Mediterraneans who settled in Northwest Africa.

EUROPEAN NATIONS IN NORTHWEST AFRICA, 1954

French		Spanish	
Algeria	850,000	Algeria	40,000
Morocco	300,000	Morocco	300,000
Tunisia	150,000	Tunisia	10,000
Total	1,300,000	Total	350,000

Italian	
Algeria	20,000
Morocco	15,000
Tunisia	85,000
Total	120,000

French citizenship carried more weight and privilege because France installed itself in Algeria as early as 1830, and later became the protector power in Tunis (1881) and Morocco (1912).

The Population Division

Some 450,000 Jews inhabited Northwest Africa in 1955, ranging in economic status from the poorest menial workers to powerful business or professional leaders. After 1870, with the exception of the Vichy anti-Jewish legislation (1942-1944), Algerian Jews enjoyed full French citizenship granted by the Crémieux law. Jews living in Tunisia and Morocco traditionally possessed fewer rights and privileges, but it is an error to consider their condition as hopeless, or that of a persecuted minority in an Arab sea. Arab and Jew for the most part lived and worked under reasonably harmonious circumstances.

With the creation of the independent states of Morocco, Tunisia, and Algeria, important numbers of Jews—those identifying with the colonials—emigrated. The Jewish presence in Northwest Africa preceded the European by centuries and its history was more complex. Some indigenous Jewish families shared the habitat with the Berbers, and were among the earliest people to be mentioned in recorded history. Doubtless some were Berber converts to Judaism before the Roman invasions. Others came to Northwest Africa when they were driven from Spain at the time of the Christian reconquest during the late Middle Ages. Some specialists in commerce arrived from Leghorn during the eighteenth century. Finally, Jews came to Northwest Africa in the nineteenth century with the French, Spanish, and Italian colonizers, as well as from the Mediterranean islands of Malta, Majorca, and Corsica. That many North African Jews were highly educated, skilled citizens who played an important role in the business, professions, and governments of their countries, requires little emphasis. The basis of independent Morocco's opposition to the emigration of the Moroccan Jews in answer to Ben Gurion's Zionist call is that Morocco needs these talented inhabitants for its own development.

Well over 95 per cent of the inhabitants of North Africa are Muslims, a word which denotes their Islamic religious affiliation. The name "Muslim" is nearly synonymous with the word "Arab," since almost all Arabs are Muslims. The reverse, that all Muslims in the area are Arabs, is less true. Such a proposition overlooks the Berber base of the Northwest African population.

The Berbers came to the Maghrib at least as early as the second millennium B.C., sixteen centuries before the Arab conquest. Their precise origins are still a mystery, but it is judged that they came from the east, perhaps the Red Sea area or Egypt, possibly farther. They pushed as far west as the Canary Islands whose early people spoke a primitive Berber tongue called Guanche. Berber is almost always a spoken language, Hamitic in class, which tells us that it relates to ancient Egyptian and is probably closer to Semitic than to the Indo-European languages. Today approximately one-quarter of the Muslim population speak Berber, while the remainder use Arabic. A considerable number of city and town-dwelling Muslims also speak French. Spanish and Italian are less frequently employed second languages.

Important Berber communities exist in Morocco and Algeria, in contrast to Tunisia, where almost no Berbers remain. The largest concentration is in the central and southern Atlas mountains of Morocco, with a less numerous group in the Rif. In Algeria, the Kabylia and the Aurès mountains have always been Berber strongholds. Further east, in Libya and Egypt, additional Berber communities thrive, and some eke out a precarious living in the Sahara.

Anthropologists tell us that the Berbers are not an ethnically homogeneous race. But scholars agree that they are white, most frequently dark-eyed, with a liberal sprinkling of blue-eyed and green-eyed types who usually have blondish or reddish hair. Some, like the Tuareg of the south, possess tall, stately bodies with elongated heads, while in the Rif and Kabylia regions the Berber type is short, round-headed, and hard to distinguish from the stocky southern European.

Historians of the Maghrib constantly note the ability of the Berbers to withstand assimilation by the various conquerors who came to the south shores of the Mediterranean. By retreating into the mountains or the desert and making lightning thrusts into the plains for food or booty, these people maintained their personality and their customs. Even today in the Berber areas of Morocco and Algeria, clan and tribal custom hold precedence over Islamic law. These historians also note the Berber love of freedom and democratic practice. This tendency stems in part from the custom of allowing the male heads of the family to meet for major local decisions in the *Jemaa* or tribal council. But whether or not this institution reinforced the democratic or the oligarchic principal, it served as a powerful and effective check on one-man rule. Carried to excess, these practices resulted in what some writers call "Berber anarchy." Though they inhabited the same area for centuries, the Berbers rarely organized a state of their own with particular cultural characteristics. Instead they accepted a state hegemony usually provided by the conquering people, whether Carthaginian, Roman, or Arab.

Beginning in the seventh century the Arabs drove into Berber North Africa. Berber resistance, far more stubborn than that of the Byzantines, finally broke, at least to the point of accepting Islam and the Arabic language. Again in the eleventh century the Arabs swarmed over the Maghrib, as Ibn Khaldun put it, "like an army of locusts." Once more the process of Arabization moved forward, although the Berbers still maintained much of their racial independence. Widespread intermarriage has gradually produced a large Arabized Berber population which one still finds today.

There is still much Berber influence in contemporary North Africa. The differences or rivalries, however, between Arabs and the Arabo-Berber population on one hand, and the traditional Berbers on the other, is not constant. Historically, they stood together against outside forces, such as the Portuguese effort to establish footholds along the Atlantic coast of Morocco in the fifteenth and sixteenth centuries. In the recent Algerian independence struggle (1954-1962) the Berbers fought the French just as fiercely and effectively as the Arabs or the Arabo-Berbers. The autochthonous people—that is, the people who had traditionally lived in North Africa, as distinct from the recent European invaders—closed ranks and strongly supported the cause of national independence, even though their French governors said they were not a nation and tried to pit them against each other. Although the winning of Algerian independence required such an enormous joint effort, once the battle had been won old antagonisms quickly rose to the surface.

Arabization

In recent years Arabization has proceeded rapidly in Morocco and it promises to move with speed in independent Algeria. One must remember that the French tried to rule by dividing Arabs and Berbers, by an exaggeration of their differences and antagonisms. In Morocco, for example, the French provided segregated schools for the Berbers. They tried, unsuccessfully in the long run, to rally the interior tribes to the tricolor behind Al-Glawi, a powerful Berber caid (tribal leader) whose base was Marrakech. The importance of the Berbers to Moroccan unity was clearly demonstrated by Al-Fassi's visits to the tribesmen of the Middle Atlas, when he emphasized the common history of Arab and Berber to win them over to Istiqlal, the Independence Party. Douglas Ashford reminds us that "the percentage of population that has joined Istiqlal is smaller in the Berber-speaking areas," in a thirteen to nineteen ratio. Unlike the early history of independent Algeria, Morocco evolved upon a multi-party base and in 1959 the Popular Movement took legal form as a rural or tribesmen's party. It is extremely premature to assess continuing Berber influence upon the Kingdom of Morocco and the Democratic and Socialist Republic of Algeria. They are states which are opening new chapters in their history.

Independence of Morocco and Algeria, one may speculate, will bring increasing Arabization. As the French rulers tried to stamp it out or ignore it, the new states will use it both as policy and means. The enormous efforts being made in both countries to combat illiteracy will soon bring spoken and written Arabic, and French, into the remotest hamlet. Spoken Berber will surely continue, but its utility may well be reduced. The drive toward development and modernization could have a similar result, but Berber customs and practices surely will survive and be honored. The beautiful hand-craft work, the colorful rugs, will be sought after by the visitor from the outside world. But the tools and the necessities of modernization seem to bypass the Berber language and customs. The press toward the cities has a similar effect. Islam in its various forms will continue to exert a strong influence on North Africa. Although Algerian leaders can speak of a secular attitude, Muslim religion is increasing all over Africa and certainly not diminishing in the Maghrib, though it is being adapted toward modern life. It might well be, then, that Islam and the Arabic language will be even more important in the future than they have been in the recent colonial past. The leaders in all these states are Arab or Arabo-Berber in outlook and conviction. They see their states as integrally independent, but sympathetic, first, to the Arabic world, then, to the African continent, and finally, to the whole world.

The economy of Northwest Africa from Roman times to the coming of the Europeans in the nineteenth century rested upon the struggle for subsistence. It was primitive, backward by Western standards, and in the fifteen hundred years before 1830, small effort had been made to change or improve it. While Europe applied the results of the scientific and technological revolutions to agriculture, industry, and commerce, the Maghribi followed the traditional route of hand to mouth, using archaic tools and methods, producing scarcely enough to create a local market, if that. How could such a dismal situation derive from a civilization which offered so much to medieval science, music, and architecture? A full explanation of this question would necessitate an exploration of North African history since the seventh century.

We can see clearly enough in general outline, however, that society was frozen, that the incentives which prevailed in Europe were lacking. Isolationism worked to keep out those foreign ideas and practices which would have been most beneficial; there was nothing in Islam remotely resembling the material predestination of a doctrine like Calvinism, which some scholars related to the growth of capitalism in the West. "Enterprise," in the sense that this word took on such important meaning in Modern Europe, could not be found in the Maghrib. Nor was there any state of the absolute-mercantilist variety so characteristic of Europe. These and many other reasons may be adduced to the question.

The European "Invasion"

The hard fact is that first the agricultural and then the industrial revolution came to this area with Europeans, already long familiar with such dynamic forces. Thus, an archaic, backward economy resting upon barter, scarcity, feeble exploitation, and with almost no trade or commerce fell under the penetrating European eye, which was looking eagerly for new areas of exploitation. The traditional Maghribi economy whose stability, or stagnation, rested upon the precarious balance between weak agricultural productivity and a stable population, was invaded, sometimes violently, by a band of Europeans with a totally different outlook. Devoted to a capitalism which boomed or sagged at home, the Europeans "arrived in the Maghrib with development, capital, plenty of ideas, much initiative, not many scruples, and the conviction that they could behave in Africa as they had in Europe." [2] Their prime purpose was to make Africa yield as much as Europe; one condition favored this hope: labor was cheap.

This clash produced unforeseen results. An enormous change took place in the Maghrib from Tunis to Tangier, as Europeans modern-

[2] Le Tourneau, p. 33.

ized and transformed the area. Highways, railroads, steamship lines, airports, electric circuits, telephones, automobiles, and much more bore the European imprint. Subsoil resources (the phosphates in Morocco, the iron ore in the Gafsa region of Tunisia, oil, natural gas, and minerals of the Algerian Sahara) were found and used. Schools and hospitals took form. Dams and hydroelectric power plants were built by men who sought solutions to the irrigation problem. Soil reclamation and rural amelioration programs found their way, in the twentieth century, to the resisting, stoic Muslim farmers. Resistance was easy to explain. These reforms and instruments of progress came from the hand of the conqueror and hence were suspect. The reforms themselves violated the established ways of life.

No one, not even the most militant nationalist from Morocco, Algeria or Tunisia, can deny the European genius or imprint. It practically wiped out the weaker traditional economy in its drive to develop, transform and modernize North Africa for a profit. When it placed the traditional hand-skilled artisan, for example, in front of a machine, it imposed an absolutely traumatic situation upon him that had the immediate result of reducing employment. Think of the profound disorientation of millions of Algerians who left their villages and went to France to find work without any preparation for what they were going to experience. "Just try to imagine the daring these men needed to launch out into the unknown when many of them had never seen an automobile or a railway, or even a water tap or a staircase." [3]

Behind the fact that in 1954 thirty-five power stations in Algeria generated 800,000,000 kilowats of electricity to drive some 600 industrial plants which each employed more than fifty men, there lay a marvelous and sometimes grim story. In the minds of the European shareholders, engineers, enterprisers, managers, and ultimate consumers, a primitive land was transformed, rebuilt. French genius was at its best; light replaced darkness, progress conquered backwardness. The *bidet* came to North Africa. The Algerian bourgeois who traditionally lived in the city and who could afford and understand this supply of energy, agreed with this evaluation. The Berber villager or tribesman high in the Grand Kabylia or Aurès had no opinion; he did

[3] Germaine Tillion, *Algeria, The Realities* (New York, Knopf, 1958), p. 71.

not know what electricity was. Perhaps his son, a member of the urban unemployed, resented this European achievement because he could neither share it nor take any pride in its creation and operation. He stood outside, ready to come in, uninvited, and therefore a likely subject for conversion either to Marxism or to a nationalistic movement, often to both.

What did the few Algerian students who were lucky enough to reach Paris think? They wanted their own carbon copy of this fabulous city with its particular life. They thought it would be wonderful to transform their country and people, with benefit of European science and technology, into an independent state. They wanted, for brothers and sisters left behind in Algeria, the material possessions and opportunities found in France. So the students set about their training, preparing for the day when they would be prepared to move into the twentieth century and become the business, professional, and political leaders in Algeria.

A similar attitude prevailed among the Algerian workers and the less numerous Moroccans and Tunisians who came to France. They worked hard for the minimum wages of the unskilled. They lived miserably, frequently ruining their health, and they sent money home to help their families. They lived in hope of a better day when they might return to the sun, and work for Algeria, Morocco, or Tunisia, independent and proud.

Yet the picture of Northwest Africa in modern times, as an area in which all the Europeans exploited the indigenous land and people to amass wealth, is not an accurate or fair one. Nor were all the Muslims either in rags eating their seed crops in the rural areas or working as porters and shoe-shine boys in the cities. Such a black and white analysis demands modification.

In the cities there evolved a class of "poor whites" who lacked education or refinement and whose livelihood depended upon manual or unskilled labor. Proud of their European citizenship, these "poor whites" were favored before the law in comparison to the Muslims no matter what education or background the latter might have. This class of whites associated itself whole-heartedly with the "civilizing mission" of France. Unfortunately they contributed little to it but chauvinism and racism.

WINGATE COLLEGE LIBRARY
WINGATE, N. C.

Because of the unequal social situation in Algeria, the "poor whites" enjoyed a status superior to the one they might aspire to in France, Spain, or Italy where they or their fathers and grandfathers were born. In Europe, rivalry with their own kind would take on a severity unknown in Africa, where they could literally "lord it over" the natives. Cab drivers, clerks, *bistro* owners, lower governmental employees, these people felt they would lose status and income should the Muslims be given educational opportunities or full citizenship. So they resisted change, sang the *Marseillaise* the loudest, and rebelled in the streets when a governor general or a minister from Paris suggested an amelioration in the lot of the indigenous people lower on the totem pole.

In the modern history of the Maghrib, Muslim society, though relatively closed to the outsider, contained a great internal range. Although many Muslims lived at the subsistence level, or below, a small and affluent scholar and commercial class lived in the cities. In the rural areas social organization frequently was tribal or took the form of clans. In the clans there were heads of numerous families, generally owning land or land privileges commensurate with the number of their male relatives. There were chiefs, religious leaders, and famous fighters, all with differing social status and degrees of wealth. Wealth, sometimes measurable in camels, horses, farming and grazing land, might depend on the season or the success or failure of "neighborly" raids. Prestige, or perhaps it is better to say honor, resided in the man himself and was often reflected in the conduct of the tribe or clan. Some groups lived a nomadic life. Others, like the Shawia of the Aurès, lived in a closed economy, which combined agriculture and stock raising. The Shawia men performed the heavy work and the women specialized in handicraft. Often women had much influence in the raising of the children. No single social system dominated. People like the Mozabites faced the "challenge of the desert" in their five cities in ways different from those of the Kabyles further to the north.

These isolated rural dwellers knew almost nothing of the ways of the West, even during the late years of the French period. Germaine Tillion, the brilliant ethnographer at the Sorbonne, found that in the remote villages of the Aurès in the 1930's one never saw a French teacher or medical officer; once in two or three years a bewildered gendarme or two might wander inoffensively through the region. This means that the bulk of these rural people have yet to discover the twentieth century or the role expected of independent states. They will probably not be allowed by their new leaders to cling to the old ways; at the same time they are far from prepared, or willing, to move rapidly into the modern world.

With the nascent Muslim middle class, the story differs. Its members took on countless European ways. In recent times many of the Muslim bourgeoisie believe in a modern western education for their sons, and willingly grant their daughters some voice in the selection of a husband. The older urban family circle, where the parents, children, wives, and grandchildren all lived in a tight compound enclosing a courtyard and a fountain, slowly became more modern and less religiously orthodox. The changing mores and customs of women have particularly brought them more fully into the world.

Political attitudes of the Muslim bourgeois varied greatly according to time and circumstance, but certainly he knew more about Europe and the West than the rural dweller. Sometimes he studied in Paris, did business with Europeans, and frequently functioned for the French administration. When war came he served as a "noncom" or in rare cases as an officer. When nationalist revolution rent past conceptions of living, he might press for moderate goals, favoring an evolutionary approach. But as time passed, he had to choose between France and his North African "*patrie*." For the Moroccan and Tunisian Muslim bourgeois, who never really lost his national identity, the choice was simple. He *was* a North African. The Algerian was forced to make a more complicated decision. The *beni oui oui*, the French "yes man," and the *harki* in the French army made a decision to serve France, but many bourgeois Muslims and almost all the intellectuals and members of the liberal professions rallied to the nationalist banner.

The Europeans broke down the traditional Muslim barriers. In 1830 a European in Morocco needed the express permission of the sultan to ride horseback. Thirty-five years later the Béclard Convention exempted Muslims under the protection of Europeans from the jurisdiction of the *Makhzan*, the traditional Moroccan central government.[4] All this, and much more of the same occurred long before France declared a protectorate in Morocco (March 30, 1912). This codified the policy of penetration. At the same time, with German approval, after the Franco-German Convention (November 4, 1911), it removed the Moroccan question from the crisis-laden diplomacy of pre-World War I Europe.

Morocco's economic importance to Europe had earlier been highlighted during the Crimean War (1854-1856), when France and Britain supported Ottoman Turkey against Tsarist Russia. The latter power, long the supplier of wheat to Eastern Europe, could not perform this service when the Baltic and Black Seas fell under Anglo-French naval control. This circumstance coinciding with a series of poor harvests in Eastern Europe and the heavy demand to feed the Anglo-French expedition in the Crimea, resulted in scarcity and rapidly rising wheat prices on the continent. Acting under orders of their respective war ministries, French and British businessmen in Morocco purchased large quantities of cereals and woolens. Moroccan seaports thrived.

> In the winter of 1855-1856 . . . the Atlantic port of Mazagan, whose export grain shipments had quadrupled over the last three years, accommodated 128 ships in four months. At Casablanca in one day 28 ships awaited their cargo.[5]

Long before French Northwest Africa supplied troops to the trenches of the Marne and Oise and the eastern frontier fortresses of World War I, the area had become a war time asset.

All along the Maghrib west from the Tunisian peninsula, the Europeans moved into the coastal strip, building as they advanced. Cities like Algiers and Casablanca became showplaces where the visitor could see the results of wonderful and fearless enterprise. Most of these showcase cities were two cities: one in which Conrad Hilton offered concrete, glass, and exquisite service; the other "the native quarter," the *bidonvilles* (tin can towns) in which most of the Mus-

---

[4] Jean-Louis Miège, *Le Maroc et l'Europe* (1830-1894) (Paris: Presse Universitaires de France, 1961), II, pp. 401-409.

[5] Miège, II, pp. 298-99.

lims lived. This tremendous contrast is of prime importance in understanding the political evolution of the last decades.

It explains in large part why the "natives" were not grateful for the luxury and modernity which Europeans brought to their countries. If a real renascence existed, why did the indigenous people and their leaders drive toward independence? Again, the answer is far from complex. The Europeans built primarily for themselves. The indigenous people, rightly or wrongly, felt left out.

In Algeria in 1954, before the revolution which led to independence began, Europeans owned almost all the best land and one-third of the total surface. How they got it is a complicated tale of conquest, forced purchase, seizure for penalties, and legitimate possession. Industry, too, and profits were in the same hands in larger proportion, approximately 92 per cent. Educational opportunities were, essentially, open to European youths and closed to the Muslims. In 1954 one Muslim boy in five and one Muslim girl in sixteen attended school. Four-fifths of the students at the University of Algiers were Europeans.

In Morocco in 1958, two years after independence, a young Columbia University-trained Moroccan economist, Umar Elhanjia, occupying a vital government post, was proudest of the progress his country had made in opening educational opportunities for Moroccan youth. "Yes," he said, "the French say we are going to the dogs. They were here forty years. And at the end there were 200,000 Moroccan children in school. We have been here for two years and 500,000 children attend classes." By 1959 the figure reached 700,000.

It really made little difference to the Muslim inhabitants of Northwest Africa if the Europeans constructed luxury hotels or villas; they alone lived in them. What the people of the Maghrib desperately wanted was status. They found themselves reduced to inferiority in their own countries and saw their leaders become subordinate to European governor generals. This led to a continuous restlessness which is not hard to discover if one probes beyond the official statements of the Europeans.

British Consul Sir William Henry Haggard witnessed the hooting and booing of French Resident René Millet in 1895 in Tunisia. Millet was traveling around to explain the virtues of conscription to the Tunisians. At one point he clinched his argument by noting that the Tunisians "had been brought to order *à coup de canon*. This provoked a perfect outburst of yells and the Resident was furiously hooted as we rode away." Later at the ceremonies attending the opening of the port of Sfax, Haggard observed the difficulties experienced by the French in rounding up even this captive audience. The Arabs "were quite silent; if sitting or lying down they did not rise, and if they saluted with their hands at all, which was infrequent, it was with an indifferent nonchalance which showed pretty clearly" their feelings. One of the French officers later told Haggard that it was "only with the greatest difficulty that the Arabs were induced to come at all, that they had . . . absolutely refused to take any part in the proceedings." After urgent and violent threats by their caid who himself was sent by the French authorities "to compel their appearance . . . they finally consented to pass *en bloc* before the Tribune in which were seated representatives of their conquerors." [6]

The European presence in Northwest Africa in the nineteenth century accomplished many fine things for the Europeans; yet its structure contained a lethal flaw. This was the European settler or planter (colon) who came to stay and to exploit the area in quest of personal wealth, which he soon used to acquire political power. Colon influence was two-fold: in the colony or protectorate he exercised his power through economic and social position, and at home in Paris he represented the colony in such a way as almost to ignore the existence of the indigenous population. The colon became the road block preventing the fulfillment of the Muslim dream of status and equality. It was the frustration of this dream after World War II that led to the struggle for independence.

For many years this duality has been clearly understood by well-informed students. Writing in 1887, Paul Leroy-Beaulieu, a professor of political economy in the Collège de France, noted that this position of the indigenous population of Algeria weakened when French colons represented Algeria in the Chamber of Deputies in Paris. From

---

[6] The quotations from Consul Haggard's reports are in Nicola A. Ziadeh, *Origins of Nationalism in Tunisia* (Beirut: American University, 1962), p. 60, citing F.O. 27/3237, Haggard to Kimberly, March 15, 1895 and F.O. 27/3345, Haggard to Salisbury, April 30, 1895.

the French viewpoint Algeria was "an integral part of France," administratively speaking.

The entry into Parliament since 1871 of deputies representing the colons has singularly prejudiced the situation of the indigenous African population. . . . The French administration has become and becomes each day less protective and less impartial. . . . For this single reason government practices are today more adverse to the indigenous population than before 1870.[7]

Three years later, in 1900, Sir Ernest Berkeley, the British Consul in Tunis, made a similar judgment and accompanied it with a wise guess.

I am disposed to think that the advent of a really "colon" policy must herald the ruin of, or at least the gravest danger to, the Regency's future chances of prosperity. It already suffers not a little from the incidence of heavy taxation and the burden of an immoderately large administration. Were French "colonial" aspirations to be realized . . . I more than doubt that the Regency, or France itself, could eventually be anything but losers.[8]

[7] Quoted from *L'Algérie et la France* (Paris, 1887) by Jacques Fonlupt Esperaber in Simone de Beauvoir and Gisèle Halimi, *Djamila Boupacha* (Paris: Gallimard, 1962), pp. 247-48.
[8] Ziadeh, citing F.O. 27/3506 Berkeley to Salisbury, December 9, 1900, p. 57.

TWO

NORTHWEST AFRICA

BEFORE THE CONQUEST

The full sweep of recorded history in Northwest Africa conveys to its reader succeeding pictures of invasion and infiltration of peoples from the Near East, the Mediterranean, and Europe. In comparison to this multiplicity of influence, entry of men and ideas from the desert south has been relatively unimportant. There are, however, some inhabitants of today's Maghrib who came from the sub-Sahara zone. Of course, most parts of the world with long recorded histories, whether in Europe or Asia, have been subject to important invasions shaping their institutions, the mentality of their leadership, and their posture in today's world. Our task is to evaluate the impact of these movements, to separate the influences, and to judge them in the modern context.

In the case of Northwest Africa, the Berber peoples sustained five major thrusts from the outside and many minor ones. The Phoenician and the Carthaginian imprint lasted a millennium from approximately 1200 B.C. Carthaginian civilization, which was more advanced, made a deep impression upon the Berber world. The Punic language, developed from Phoenician and closely related to Hebrew, was "as near Arabic as Spanish is to French," and this linguistic relationship may explain the later rapid spread of Arabic culture. It is certainly one reason why Berber became much more rare in Tunisia (Carthage), the Punic main base, than in peripheral Algeria and Morocco.

Rome's imprint was felt in 146 B.C., with the fall of Carthage, and lasted uninterruptedly for nearly seven centuries. Today the casual traveler can find almost as many Roman ruins between Libya and Volubilis in Morocco as in the French Midi. Roads, monuments, dams, bridges all in the Roman repertoire, dotted Northwest Africa, some of whose inhabitants joined Roman society. Emperor Septimus Severus was an African. St. Augustine, who profoundly moved the Christian world from Hippo (Bône, Algeria) with his intellect and heart, may have been a Punic or a Berber. Like the French almost two thousand years later, the Romans found it extremely difficult to subduc the Berbers of the Aurès mountains.

Vandals and Byzantines filled the gap left by an enervated Rome. For a two-century interregnum (429-642), between the death of Europe's greatest empire and the first arrival of the Arabs, new outside influences, German tribesmen entering Africa from Spain and Byzantines disembarking from the Mediterranean, flooded into Roman Africa. Apart from blood mixture through marriage with the indigenous population and the influence of Byzantine architecture upon many a later mosque, the Vandal and Byzantine impact upon latter day civilization in Northwest Africa was relatively minor.

If, after the Romans, the Vandal and Byzantine influence appears something of an anti-climax, the opposite is true of the Arab invasions. By A.D. 642, ten years after the death of the Prophet Mohammed, the vanguard of the Arabic invasions reached Libya, beginning a political conquest which lasted twelve centuries in Morocco and eight centuries in the remainder of Northwest Africa. When the French obtained a protectorate in Morocco early in the twentieth century, or when the Ottoman Turks displaced Arab rule in Algeria and Tunisia early in the sixteenth (themselves to be displaced by the French in the nineteenth century), there were important political changes. They made, however, small difference to the culture of the people.

The Arabic language and the Islamic religion remained deeply imbedded in the people of Northwest Africa. Arabic and Islam surely were no more sophisticated than Latin or Christianity, yet they achieved a permanent status where these earlier influences had passed away. The Berber population must have been more receptive to the Arab way of life than the European. Why?

One may guess that the message of the surging Arabs was heard and understood, spoken as it was in a more flexible language than Latin and one closer to the Berber. The young religion, which had appealing human qualities, pleased them. Its concepts conformed more closely to their life and way of thinking. Arab administration was less formal, less bureaucratic and imposing than the Roman, and this suited the clan government of the Berbers. The Romans, and later the French, tried to assimilate the peoples of Northwest Africa; the Arabs came with kindred institutions and struck a receptive balance between the gifts they brought and those they accepted. An equity prevailed between Berber and Arab which Berber and Roman or European did not attain. Both came as conquerors. The one was rejected and turned away, only to return centuries later. The other remained, intermarried, implanted its language, religion, architecture, and literature. Romans and Europeans felt themselves expatriates in Northwest Africa; the Arabs were at home.

European development itself between the collapse of the Roman Empire and the advent of the Crusades in the late eleventh century facilitated the Arabization of Northwest Africa. In those centuries, Europe, preoccupied at home with trying domestic challenges and defending its interest from the Norse and Slavs, withdrew from the southern shore of the Mediterranean. In contrast the Arabs pressed all the way to Poitiers in central France, and later settled down in Spain, from which peninsula they were not entirely expelled until the century of America's discovery.

The Arab Assimilation

The salient fact is that after the seventh century the people of Northwest Africa turned toward the Arabic life and fixed their eyes upon Mecca. Not really until the nineteenth century did Europe have another chance to expend political energy upon the Northwest African strip. And once again this political penetration was rejected. Possibly the European (French) cultural legacy in independent Morocco, Algeria, and Tunisia will become a more respected gift when it is no longer proffered on the end of a bayonet. Such a speculation time alone must evaluate.[1]

[1] David C. Gordon, *North Africa's French Legacy 1954-1962* (Cambridge, Mass.: Harvard University Press, 1962), pp. 65-84.

If the Arabic language and Islam took root in Northwest Africa more deeply than the culture of previous invaders, this result was partly due to the technique of Arab imperialism. Instead of settling colonists, as had the Romans and the later French, who symbolized a stronger, alien civilization, the Arabs furthered their influence by founding a ruling class from descendants of marriages between Arab leaders and local women. This imperialism of "blood fusion" was so generally practiced, that after a few generations the leaders, Arabic in spirit and culture, usually had no more than a trace of Arab blood. These dark horsemen from the desert, it is said by early historians, had a marked preference for blondes who could easily be found among the blue-eyed Berbers and the Christian slave population. It is remarked by Julien Ribera, the Spanish scholar, that the percentage of Arab blood in the veins of Caliph Abd-al-Rahman (912-961) was less than one per cent. The Caliph was 99 per cent Spanish.[2] Arab imperialism was not based upon racial supremacy or upon superior cultural attributes. It entered by force and impressed its culture because it appreciated what it found and did not fear that its ideas would become diluted by blood ties.

From the beginning, too, of Arab expansion to the northwest, local governors resented, and soon shook off the authority exerted from Damascus. Yet these same governors and their subjects looked in that direction for religious guidance and cultural development. But they refused, as do the leaders of the contemporary independent Maghrib, to accept the political control of the Near East (or Cairo). Brothers, yes; subjects, no.

In Northwest Africa the Arab presence moved first upon the Exarchate of Carthage which fell permanently in 698. A few years later, in 710, a Berber lieutenant named Tarif reached Andalusia in Spain. A year later, with a force of perhaps eight thousand men (mostly Berbers) another leader, Tarik, captured the pillar of Hercules and called it Djebel Tarik (the rock of Tarik), later corrupted to "Gibraltar." Visigothic power in Spain, weakened by religious conflict which involved severe persecution of Christian heretics and Jews, quickly collapsed under the assault of the Arabo-Berber forces.

[2] Cited by Nevill Barbour, ed., A Survey of North West Africa (The Maghrib) (London: Oxford University Press, 1959), p. 16.

Spain, with the exception of the mountainous areas in Galicia and Asturias in the northwest, fell to invaders who often placed the recently persecuted Jews in command of captured towns. By 725 Arab forces crossed the Pyrenees into France, only to be checked seven years later by Charles Martel near Poitiers.

Arab culture and power in the Maghrib centered for many centuries in southern Spain—Córdoba and Seville became "western Bagdads"—and in "Ifriqiya" (the Arabic version of the Roman name for "Africa," meaning Carthage). From the new capital city of Kairouan, and later from Tunis, rulers usually commanded not only Tunisia but also eastern Algeria and Tripolitania. Western Algeria most frequently fell under administration from Morocco.

Though the culture of Tunis reflected in its maturity the direct influences of the Punic and Roman past, the Arabic period of its history combined expansionist ambition with violence. Under the Aghlabid dynasty in the ninth century, Sicily was conquered. The Fatimid dynasty of the next century moved the capital to Mahdiya, conquered Egypt, and created a Shiah Caliphate in Cairo, from whence Tunisia itself was ruled by tributaries, the Zirids. The latter, in asserting their independence of Cairo, brought upon themselves the invasion of the Beni Hilal and the Beni Sulaim. These were brigand bedouin peoples, good examples of "non-assimilating" Arabs whom Ibn Khaldun, the Arab historian, disparaged. This army did very little but destroy and pillage, ruining the great city of Kairouan and often serving as a mercenary force in local tribal and dynastic feuds. Momentarily, in the twelfth century, the Normans controlled part of the coastline. At this time the Arabized Berber dynasty, the Almohades from Morocco, gained control of the back country.

In the thirteenth century stability and growth returned when a dissident Almohad governor founded the Hafsid dynasty. For a period of two hundred years culture flourished. It was in part the result of an influx of superior artisans and scholars, refugees from Muslim Spain. Tunis once again became a thriving city with a vibrant urban culture whose influence stretched to the smaller towns.

By the end of the fifteenth century this flowering ceased, as the Hafsids fell under combined attacks from Christian Spain and the Ottoman Turks. Imperial cares weakened the Spanish effort under

Charles V; and the Ottoman Turks filled the power vacuum, soon extending their sway to the frontier of Morocco. Ifriqiya, administered from Constantinople in three *ojaks* (regencies)—Tripoli, Tunis, and Algiers—at first fell under strict Turkish military rule. These units corresponded closely to the frontiers of the later twentieth-century independent states of Libya, Tunisia, and Algeria. The Turkish ruling caste in Tunis, however (never more than a slender minority), soon developed independent habits. Constantinople, separated by great distances, and deeply engaged in Eastern Europe, in the Black Sea area, and in the Persian frontier, granted the autonomy of its domain in Northwest Africa. A Turkish Janissary born in Crete established the Husainid dynasty in 1705 and called himself Bey. From that time until the creation of the French protectorate in 1881 the Beys continued to rule along Turkish politico-military lines. Tunisian liberal forces raised demands for a constitution in 1856, but this effort proved stillborn. It reflected, however, the influence of European political thought—the first of its kind in an Arab country. And the word *Destour*, Constitution, found its way into the name of future nationalist movements. The Husainid dynasty experienced increasingly difficult financial problems as the nineteenth century passed its midpoint, and these, unsolved, helped to pave the way for the French protectorate. The Husainid dynasty formally survived the protectorate, but gave way in 1957 when independent Tunisia became a republic.

In the many centuries before the protectorate, Tunisia (Carthage) had known greatness and despair, prosperity and misery, Semitic and European influences, urban and nomadic populations often at odds. By 1881 Tunisia, with all its past greatness, stood defenseless against a predatory, expansionist Europe.

The Arab penetration of Morocco (*al-Maghrib al-Aqsa*), the "Far West," soon made it a staging area for the invasion of Spain and France. Later, as the Christian forces drove the Muslims from Spain, the refugees carried with them many superior techniques assimilated on the European continent. In Andalusia (*al-Andalus*) a truly remarkable culture flourished. We are accustomed to note the civilizing mission of Córdoba upon Western Europe, but we should not forget that the same influence filtered south into Morocco.

By the twelfth century, Arab writers noted the work of the Muslim refugees from Spain. They vitalized agriculture by locating new sources of water and preserving them. Trees were planted to hold rainfall in the soil and to prevent erosion. At the same time, artisans brought their skills into the cities, and educated administrators applied their talents.

Though the Arabs first reached Morocco perhaps in 684, not for some four hundred years did they more than touch the coastal surface. The Berber majority nominally allowed Islam to replace their animistic religions, but the Berbers had no difficulty in perpetrating their independent ways and their decentralized political institutions. The traditional unit of the non-nomadic Berbers was the "fraction," a village of sometimes a hundred or two living units, whose inhabitants came from a common family tree. The men sat in an assembly which took charge of such important matters as justice, welfare, and defense. Among the nomadic Berbers, various factions formed tribes whose leadership was loose and undefined, except in time of war.

Into this primitive but basic culture the Muslim refugees from Spain could not penetrate either rapidly or deeply, even though many carried Berber blood in their veins. And between Arab and Berber, while some linguistic and religious base for cooperation prevailed, there was also a serious rivalry which negated political unity. Nor did peace prevail within the three large tribal families—the Masmouda, the Sanhaja, and the Zenata.

Life for many centuries in Morocco involved constant violence. Tradition and the wisdom of scholars labeled the Moroccans as great fighters who "kill a man as easily as a sparrow." The wise men attributed this to climate. Similar authorities, reinforced by the record, found the Tunisians, on the contrary, a gentle, mild-mannered people.

A quick glance at Moroccan history between the eighth and seventeenth century, illustrates the great vitality of its people whose prowess made them masters of a far-flung empire. The area of battle covered a great triangle whose angles at the extreme limits were Morocco, Spain, and Tripoli. By the late eighth century, Arab Idrissites reached some ascendancy inside Morocco in the tug-of-war against the Berber groups. Moulay Idriss even found time to begin the beautiful city of Fez. Soon, however, the Berbers returned to the war task, and the

Sanhaja rulers, the Almoravides (the people of the *ribat*, 1093-1147), extended their sway not simply at home but also eastward to Algiers and deep into Spain. Originally nomads from the western Sahara, they followed Malikism, a stern version of Islam, which was preached in a fortress-monastery (*ribat*) in Mauretania. They founded Marra-kech and then fanned out many hundreds of miles, imposing their rule and serving as cultural middlemen between Andalusia and Mo-rocco.

By 1147 another Berber leader, Ibn Tumart, captured Marrakech and assumed the expansionist task. Aided by the Masmouda from the south, he pressed the imperial limits to Tripoli in the east, and Castile in the north. By 1162 he called himself Caliph. These Almohades (1147-1296) brought for the first time, and the last, a semblance of unity to the Maghrib.

The Merinides

Scarcely a century later a third Berber force captured Marrakech (1269). Led by Beni Merin and hence called Merinides, 1269-1465, they were loyally seconded by the Zenata tribes. The Almohad mira-cle quickly began to dissipate. Though the Merinides made Fez their capital, they found themselves unable to hold Tlemçen, located just inside today's Algerian border. Morocco became plagued as "Berber particularism" was accentuated by the *marabouts*, venerated local religious men of small education.

The Beni Hilal (brigand bedouin camel-owning nomads, who were a violently destructive force) added to the difficulties of the Merinides. We have already noted their sad influence upon Ifriqiya in the eleventh century. A century later they were fortunately defeated at Sétif, and the more troublesome exiled by the Almohad Sultan, Yaccub-al-Mansur. Later, bedouins from south Arabia reached lower Morocco via the upper fringes of the Sahara. Known as the Maaqil, they marched to the gates of Rabat, Arabizing the countryside in the course of this thirteenth-century march.

A far greater menace to the Merinides and the entire Muslim popu-lation of Morocco and Northwest Africa was generated by the revital-ized Christian offensive of the late fifteenth century. Long before the expulsion of the Muslims from Granada (January 2, 1492), Islam went over to the defensive. Tunis was the target of Louis IX's ill-fated crusade in 1270, and another force under the Duc de Bourbon moved against Mahdiya in Tunisia a century later. Commercial battles between the Italian ports and Tunis added economic fuel to the religious fires.

After the reconquest of Granada, the Portuguese and Spanish pressed into Africa. By the early sixteenth century Portugal held Mazagan, Tangier, and Ceuta, while Spain controlled Melilla, Oran, Algiers, Tunis, and Tripoli. In Morocco, the arrival of the Portuguese invoked basic internal changes.

When the Merinides and their related successors, the Beni Wattas (1456-1549), who also received the support of the Zenata tribes, failed to deliver Morocco from the Portuguese infidels, a *jihad*, or holy war, was invoked. This meant that the *marabouts* returned to influence as did the *shorfa*, descendants of the Prophet Mohammed. By 1549, the Saadians, *sharifs*, or sherifs (claimants of descent from the Prophet) came to power. The change marked a turning point in Moroccan leadership from Berber to Arab.

Even so, Berber political influence passed into Saadian hands in the form of the Makhzan, the state organization. The Berber imprint upon architecture and décor never left Morocco. The particularism and the individualism which so sharply characterized those tribes, also resisted Arabization into the twentieth century.

Saadian rule (1594-1654) scored a number of victories over expansionist Portugal and also checked Turkish predatory drives by forming a cautious alliance with the old antagonist, Spain, thereby bringing upon itself considerable prestige. Some support also came from the fact that the sultans were descendants of the Prophet. The weakness of the dynasty lay in the shortage of hard-fighting military manpower, since it lacked the strong tribal support commanded by the previous Berber leaders. Despite this lack, successful desert expeditions captured Timbuktu and Gao, bringing gold into Morocco. The dynasty could also boast that Morocco did not become a battlefield between Christian and Turk. This was no more than a mixed blessing, if not a disadvantage, because the Sherifian Kingdom became isolated from positive outside influences. In contrast to the other parts of the Maghrib, Algeria and Tunisia, Morocco remained a feudal kingdom into the twentieth century, with a prejudice against outside or modernizing forces—an attitude which has proved to be a handicap in contemporary times.

In the mid-seventeenth century Morocco returned to the brink of particularism and anarchy. In the northwest the Moriscos, three million of whom were expelled from Spain after 1610, created a corsair republic which centered at Rabat and neighboring Salé. Various strong holy men set themselves up as independent rulers in various sections, particularly in the Middle Atlas, from whence *marabouts* from Dila ruled Fez and Salé and extended their control to most of northern Morocco.

This lapse into particularism was checked by Moulay Rashid, a sherif of Tafilalet, an Alawite who claimed descent from the Prophet's son-in-law, Ali ibn Abi Talib. This extraordinary leader's career, which ended in 1672, prevented a new Berber dominated period and began the Alawite (Alouite) dynasty which has, since that time, furnished the Sultans of Morocco. His successor, Moulay Ismail (1672-1729), dedicated himself to protecting his land against the Turks, Christians, and, most seriously, against the Sanhaja Berbers of the Middle Atlas, who moved from those redoubts toward the Atlantic plains. On all fronts he checked his opponents' advances by constructing a series of fortresses and organizing a force of choice Negro troops recruited from the south.

Despite efforts of various Alawite Sultans in the later eighteenth and the nineteenth centuries to reduce anarchy, the battle could not be won. Berber tribes persisted in their independent ways, and European pressure of a political and, later, economic character moved into Morocco. Arab tribal support proved inadequate to the task of empire defense. The absence of a succession law meant that at each Sultan's death, a divisive power struggle ensued. By the end of the eighteenth century, most of southern Morocco had slipped from the Sultan's hands.

European Infiltration

In the nineteenth century, European pressure increased. In 1843, when the Algerian leader Abdelkader, who resisted the French occupation of his land, took refuge in Morocco, the Sultan proved powerless to respond. This haven itself might have provoked a French expedition and occupation had not Britain expressed disapproval. In 1859, Spain successfully occupied the small enclave of Ifni, situated on the Atlantic coast between the Moroccan frontier and Rio de Oro.

European penetration closely resembled the "partition of China" which took place at the same time. Morocco's strategic coasts on both the Atlantic and on the Mediterranean attracted the Europeans— Spain continued to occupy the northern coastal strip including Ceuta (since 1497) and Melilla, plus various islands taken in 1848. Also, the area supplied the continent with cereals and woolens at various times of crisis, as during the Crimean War. Finally, Morocco, known to possess minerals in unexploited quantity, was a prospector's delight and Spanish, French, British, and German consuls and companies took up residence. They built railroads and roads, expanded harbor facilities, lent the Sultan money, and, without charge, gave him much advice.

The Sultan's early hatred of the foreign invasion had to be tempered with his ability and resources to do anything about it. He ultimately became dependent upon the Europeans he disliked. What saved Moroccan independence more than anything else was European rivalry. In the Spanish-Moroccan war of 1859, Britain and France worked to localize and shorten the conflict. Despite the brevity of this war, Sultan Moulay Abbas signed a disastrous treaty with Leopold O'Donnell, which granted Spain enlarged *presidios* at Ceuta and Melilla, territory on the Atlantic coast, an indemnity of 105,000,000 gold francs, and the occupation of Tetuán. Shortly after this session, the Sultan sought loans in the European money market and new commercial treaties were signed.

> The war and the various conventions liquidating the Hispano-Moroccan conflict profoundly modified relations between Morocco and the powers as well as the internal situation within the Sherifian Empire. The advancement, stimulated by the growth of trade between 1832 and 1840 and by the Franco-Moroccan treaty of 1844, followed by the commercial convention of 1856, fulfilled itself: Morocco entered definitely into the European sphere of action. A new era began in which it was no longer possible for that state to return to isolation.[3]

[3] Miège, II, p. 383.

Since Morocco could no longer survive as an independent state if she remained isolated from the fast-changing world of technology, her sole chance depended on her ability to meet the new challenges—to modernize, to adapt to the new forces. Sultan Moulay Hassan (1873-1894), the last sultan of any stature before the protectorate, faced this situation by sending young Moroccans abroad to learn the new science. Unfortunately, when they returned they found no place for their knowledge, no means to adapt it to the resistant customs. The Sultan slowed the erosion of his sovereignty by obtaining a meeting at Madrid in 1880. The resulting Convention, signed by the great European powers and the United States, regulated the rights of foreigners in Morocco. What really delayed the "partition" or conquest of Morocco more than this Sultan's vigor, was continuous rivalry among the Europeans. By the twentieth century, however, outside pressures built up to the point where Morocco fell, as had Algeria in 1830 and Tunisia in 1881, into the French orbit.

Algeria, known geographically in Arabic as *al-Maghrib al-Ausat* (the Middle West) contained the same layers of civilization as Carthage and Morocco before the coming of the Arabs. Its Berber peoples made a grudging submission to Arabic force but quickly adopted the language and faith of the new political masters. Until the arrival of the Ottoman Turks, the western zone usually shared a common life, and often the same political leaders as Morocco. The eastern sector's history and institutions closely resemble those radiating from Carthage.

Turkish occupation, which began in the early sixteenth century and lasted three hundred years, developed when the Barbarossa brothers (a couple of North African corsairs) were called in by the Muslim inhabitants against the Spanish who held some coastal ports. Khair-al-Din Barbarossa received authorization from the Turkish Sultan to call himself Pasha. From Algiers he soon extended his authority to Bône and Constantine. Unlike the Spanish captains who stayed along the coast and never penetrated the interior, he pushed his control southward occupying Biskra, Touggourt, and Wargla. Later, Tlemçen became a Turkish base.

The Turks vested abolute power in the Pashas, later the Aghas, and finally the Deys. As time passed, nominal homage was paid the Sultan in Constantinople. The great problem faced by the Deys involved control of the Janissaries (the Turkish fighting force), whose loyalty was fickle but whose power was the basis of political control. Between the Janissaries and the corsair captains, whose booty furnished the state an important source of income, the Deys usually found themselves hamstrung. Half the time they died violent deaths at the hands of political rivals.

As a small ruling minority, the Turks lived by their wits. Usually they relied upon certain tribes to reinforce the Janissaries, and public offices were farmed at a price high enough to command loyalty. Interest centered upon Mediterranean commerce where privateers, operating from Algerian ports, made tidy sums and took many Christian prisoners. European powers who had given up the sport of privateering, except in time of war emergency, tried unsuccessfully to put a stop to this activity. Napoleon in 1808 drafted a plan to conquer "Barbary" by landing at Sidi-Ferruch. War in Spain, then in Russia, prevented the execution of this plan. In 1830, however, the French reviewed it. It suited their purposes very well.

At the Congress of Vienna (1815) the European powers discussed Barbary piracy, and again at the Congress of Aix-la-Chapelle, three years later, the subject arose.

Before the arrival of the French in the nineteenth century, Northwest Africa clearly bore the imprint of the Arabs. They delivered the language and the religion to the indigenous Berber peoples who received it wholeheartedly. Occasionally, technical innovation and skilled people reached the area, as during the Muslim retreat from Spain or the arrival of the Turkish administration. Compared to Europe, the area could be said to lack dynamism. Compared to the peoples of interior Africa, the Maghribi had a more varied experience, largely because they had direct access to the Mediterranean. That basin provided exchange with Europe and Asia, and, although it brought invaders, innovation sometimes came with them. Northwest Africa was much more intimately related to the march of Mediterranean civilization than Sub-Saharan Africa or, for that matter, West Africa.

During the nineteenth century large numbers of Europeans arrived, and with them came different habits of mind and the new science and technology. No amount of Arabo-Berber resistance could prevent this new influence from rubbing off.

THREE

EUROPEAN CONQUEST

1830-1912

Piracy and privateering had nothing to do with the shaping of active French interest in Algeria. Negotiations over debts had resulted, French leaders claimed, in a diplomatic affront. Reprisals led to retaliation. On June 14, 1830, a French force landed near Sidi-Ferruch, and on July 5 Algiers fell. In France Charles X's regime lasted to the end of the month, more than a coincidence to indicate that, in some degree, the invasion of Algeria marked an effort on the part of the French monarchy to divert its subjects from the unpopular domestic program.

The Beginnings of the Debt Crisis

The unsettled debt problem, which produced the military occupation, dated back to 1797, when two Jewish merchants, one in Algiers, the other at Marseilles, supplied French armies in Europe with wheat under conditions of delayed payment and high interest rates. When the merchants, Bakri and Busnach, failed to meet their obligations in Algiers, Dey Hussein took a hand. The case dragged on: the merchants would pay in Algiers when France paid off. France moved to settle the debt, and still the Dey waited for his money. By 1827 it appeared that the French and the Dey had been duped by Jacob Bakri. Furious, the Dey told Pierre Deval, French Consul in Algiers, "Am I responsible for obligations contracted by two Jewish business

houses. If the debt were due the King of France from one of my sub-
jects, justice would require him to pay within twenty-four hours."
Hussein next wrote directly to Charles X asking that Bakri be sent to
Algiers.

The final interview took place in Algiers on April 30, 1827, when
Hussein summoned Deval. "Why has your minister not written me
directly? Am I a peasant clod, a barefoot boy with muddy feet? You
are responsible for this . . . you wicked one, you infidel, you idol-
ater."

"My government will not write to you. It is useless."

Hussein, angered, ordered Deval to leave. Either the consul had
another word or possibly he moved too slowly. However it was, the
Dey sped his departure with three, quick forehand strokes with his
flyswatter. Deval wrote home that he (and France) had been swatted
and asked for severe reprisals.

France blockaded the port of Algiers for three years. The blockade
hurt France more than the Dey. Ships went aground and the crews
were killed, Algerian shore batteries used the French ships for target
practice. What hurt the French most was the cost of the blockade
which ran 7,000,000 francs per year. The original French obligations
for the supplies back in 1797 amounted to 24,000,000 francs which
France recognized as 7,000,000 in 1819, paying 4,500,000 francs and
depositing 2,500,000 francs against hopelessly tangled claims. Three
years of blockade at 7,000,000 francs per year meant that the whole
venture ran in the red.

In January, 1830, Charles X ordered an expedition against Algiers.
Britain carefully evaluated this French intention; British consuls in
Algiers had constantly advised Hussein to resist French pressure. The
French gave some thought to asking Mehemet Ali of Egypt to join
forces against Algiers, but apparently it was decided not to link the
Near Eastern Question with the Maghrib. Prince Metternich, the
Austrian statesman, wisely conjectured, "It is not for a blow from a
flyswatter that one spends 100,000,000 francs and risks 40,000 men."
What would Metternich have said had he been alive in 1960 to watch
France spend close to a billion dollars a year while maintaining an
army of a half-million men in Algeria, to keep it French?

On March 30, 1830, fully ten weeks before the French force landed near Sidi-Ferruch, a businessman from Toulon ran this note in *Le Sémaphore*.

A wholly new industry is going to open up with the war in Algeria. A merchant of Marseilles who owns a nice merchantman has fitted it out as a comfortable hotel. Persons who wish to witness the bombardment of Algeria and the disembarkation of our troops will be lodged and fed for an average price of 15 francs per day. This ship, which has been legally authorized, will stand off at a safe distance from enemy fire; it will be armed however with six cannon so as to defend itself against any corsair should it be attacked.[1]

Five days after the fall of Algiers Dey Hussein was shipped to Naples with his family, harem, and "considerable baggage." By August 16, Charles X of France left Cherbourg and his throne for England. France adopted a plan of limited occupation of the ports of Algiers, Oran, and Bône. This necessitated enlarged beachheads, so troops stayed on and a few colonists arrived. This was the beginning of French Algeria, a political unit and a concept which lasted until 1962 when Algeria obtained independence.

Fifty-one years after the capture of Algiers, France obtained a protectorate over Tunisia. That country, ruled by Beys who failed to solve internal financial problems, turned, in the 1860's, to European bankers such as Oppenheim in London and Erlanger in Paris. This hazardous turn became a necessity when the Tunisian population rebelled against new taxes. The Bey had either to cut the cloth of government to fit his purse or fill the purse from the outside. In choosing the latter course, he put up customs revenues and other taxes as security. When the debts remained unpaid, the Europeans created a debt collection commission which compounded the problem by lending more money at interest rates which sometimes reached 15 per cent.

As Tunisia sank under the debt burden, the European powers scrambled to intervene for the ostensible purpose of managing the finances and paying off obligations. France gained the initiative by recognizing British interests in the eastern Mediterranean. Bismarck, the German Chancellor, anxious to turn a France he defeated in 1870 away from thoughts of regaining Alsace-Lorraine, hit upon Tunisia as

[1] Charles-Henri Favrod, *La Révolution Algérienne* (Paris: Plon, 1959), p. v.

a place where Gallic frustration could be satisfied. Italy, eagerly desiring to recapture Carthage and whose nationals had gone to Tunisia for fortune and future empire, could not successfully oppose the French diplomatic preparation. At the Congress of Berlin (1878) Bismarck encouraged the French.

France moved quickly, with a two-pronged attack which came from Algeria via a new railroad toward Le Kef and from a sea-borne landing at Bizerte. Tunisia was unable to extricate itself from a welter of debts, and, when Khrumir tribesmen raided eastern Algeria, the Bey was charged with aggression. Bey Mohammed Sadoq (Al-Sadiq) signed the Bardo Treaty at Kassar Said on May 12, 1881. It allowed the French to overhaul Tunisian finance and to restore order. Two years later at La Marsa, a further concession placed France in control of Tunisia. The Bey agreed to undertake administrative, financial, and judicial reforms suggested by the French.

Under this arrangement the Bey remained a figurehead sovereign. The true ruler of Tunisia, in power terms, was the French Resident General. He organized and directed the major departments of government—finance, justice, commerce, education, agriculture, health, and public works. The Bey named two ministers, a powerless premier and "the minister of the pen," both hollow appointments. Local government, composed of the tribal districts under caids were left untouched, though their number was reduced and French "civil controllers," who reported to the Resident General, supervised them. Tunisia gradually came to be ruled directly from Paris through a string of resident generals.

Possibly it is true that the "Tunisian question" was opened in 1830 when France entered Algiers. One might conjecture, too, that the idea received reinforcement in some French minds after the catastrophe of 1870. In any case, the uneasy conditions in that North African state exposed it to penetration by new imperialists. What strikes the student is that by 1881, the first year when reasonably reliable statistics became available, there were "11,200 Italians, 700 French and 7,000 British nationals, of whom only 200 came from Britain, while the rest were Maltese." [2] The French minority was indeed small.

[2] Nicola A. Ziadeh, *Origins of Nationalism in Tunisia* (Beirut: American University of Beirut Publications, 1962), pp. 17-18.

Not until 1912, on the eve of World War I, did France obtain a protectorate in Morocco. As in the case of Algeria and Tunisia, internal financial problems, and political weakness, which was reflected in violence and lawlessness, exposed Morocco to the sharp eye of the empire builders of Europe. The interests of European businessmen grew throughout the nineteenth century, and a desire to protect their investments and open new possibilities strongly motivated them in the first decade of the twentieth century. As Europe moved toward more aggressive diplomacy, the Far West of the Maghrib with an Atlantic and Mediterranean coastline—the latter at its narrows at Spanish Ceuta just eight miles from Gibraltar—loomed important as a source of wealth, and increasingly, for strategic purpose.

Inside Morocco, the chain of events which led directly to the protectorate, began in 1894 when Sultan Moulay Hassan died leaving a fourteen year old son, Moulay Abd al-Aziz, as his successor. By 1901 Abd al-Aziz, possessing many necessary characteristics of a good ruler —intelligence, sympathy for his subjects—but who lacked strong will, began his personal rule. His first foray proved disastrous. He undertook a financial reform which involved abolishing two old abusive taxes before he adequately prepared a new tax based upon income from land and livestock. State revenues dropped sharply, leading to the sad cycle of deficits, loans, and guarantees, which ended with public finance resting in foreign hands.

The French and German Rivalry

Internal unrest of the tribes east of Fez, led by a pretender, resulted in military stalemate at precisely the time when France's interest in Morocco quickened. As France explored and laid claim to the Sahara, the incursion of Moroccan tribes into this southwestern sector of Algeria proved extremely bothersome. This time, instead of a wise Bismarck, seeking to divert France from war on the Rhine, there was German Emperor William II seeking his own place in the colonial sun. Already involved in sub-Saharan Africa, he stood athwart the French axis which sought to join Carthage with the Atlantic. In 1904 Britain supported France's right to preserve order and "to provide assistance for the purpose of all administrative, economic, financial, and military reforms" which might be required in Morocco.

France, however, was bound by the Entente Cordiale to recognize Spain's control of Melilla and Ceuta. Italy, too, favored the French project in return for a free hand in Tripoli. Thus, the ground was laid for the Moroccan crises, the nightmare of European diplomacy until 1912.

In 1905 William II of Germany resolved to bolster the Moroccan will to resist French penetration. Visiting Tangier, he made a series of declarations in which he referred to the Sultan as an "independent sovereign," and he strongly suggested that no reforms (French suggestions) be accepted. Fourteen states, including the United States, attended a conference at Algeciras the next year, hoping to find a way to reduce tension. That conference gave France and Spain wide and ill-defined police powers in Morocco but no protectorate. Both sides returned home happy, but the voting demonstrated clearly that Britain and Russia stood with France whose preponderant position they recognized.

Renewed incidents on the uncertain Algerian-Moroccan frontier soon enabled another French military intervention into Oujda. Later the massacre of European workers in Casablanca brought French troops into that city. Their presence led Moroccans to react against ineffective Sultan Abd al-Aziz and his brother Moulay Abd al-Hafid replaced him in 1908. This change failed to improve the internal condition, and rivalry between France and Germany again reached crisis proportions, this time over the question of deserters from the French Foreign Legion in Casablanca. By 1909 an agreement between those two nations recognized that France had special interests.

During the next two years Morocco declined rapidly as the French penetration moved into high gear. In financial and administrative questions French advisers became more numerous and active. By 1910 the Sultan called for French military support against a pretender. In Marrakech, the Glawi family, always jealous of Arab leadership, entered into negotiations with both French and German representatives.

Germany, understanding that the game in Morocco was in its last innings and that France would win, resolved to obtain some compensation. To emphasize this resolution, the gunboat *Panther*, returning from South Africa, was ordered into the port at Agadir on July 1, 1911.

France had earlier promised to cede territory in the Congo to Germany for a free hand in Morocco. *Panther's* presence was to insure a generous offer from France, not to protect the lives and property of Germans, the motive given the world. Britain, whose worst fear was that Germany would demand a holding on Morocco's Atlantic coast which could be turned into a naval base, hoped that the territory in the Congo would satisfy the Kaiser. By November 4, after four months of difficult negotiations, France and Germany agreed that Germany should receive 107,000 square miles of French Congo and that France could establish a protectorate in Morocco.

The Treaty of Fez, signed March 30, 1912, granted France a protectorate from Sultan Moulay Abd al-Hafid. The following November, Spain and France defined the limits of the Spanish zone which included Ceuta, Melilla, the Ifni enclave, and Cape Juby in the south. Spain thus held its own protectorate in northern Morocco, along both the Atlantic and Mediterranean coastlines. It was further agreed that Tangier should be internationalized, but not until 1923 did Britain, France, and Spain draft a statute.

The French Occupation

Morocco did not go as gently into the French administrative armature as Tunisia had. Berber tribesmen looked upon the new conquerors with the dislike they traditionally held for outsiders. For the Sultan whose weakness led to such humiliation, they held scorn, and Abd al-Hafid abdicated in favor of another brother soon after the Treaty of Fez. In France the diplomatic work was at an end, but the infinitely more difficult task of occupation had yet to be faced. Pierre Parent, a later deputy who represented French residents of Morocco, put the problem this way. "It is as conquerors and by force of arms that we came to Morocco and it is hypocrisy to pretend otherwise." [3]

Using the Algiers conquest of 1830 as a *point d'appui*, France had carved itself a vast empire in the Maghrib. From that center, vast stretches of the upper Sahara were explored and occupied. French interest in the border states of Tunisia and Morocco arose from the same point. By 1914, when World War I destroyed the European

[3] Pierre Parent, *Causeries sur le Maroc de 1951* (Toulouse, Imprimerie Régionale, 1951), p. 23.

equilibrium, these Northwest African holdings proved to be an important asset.

French colonial policy and administrative practice in Northwest Africa more closely resembled the Roman imperial model than the British. While it is perfectly true that a more direct administration characterized the effort in Algeria, in the protectorates of Tunisia and Morocco, the direct French system was grafted upon an indigenous base. The view prevailed that the institutions and the civilization of Paris (*mission civilisatrice*) could only be a blessing for the Arabo-Berber peoples. In the fullness of time, one great France with liberty, equality, and fraternity for all would take form. Such a long-range program depended at first upon force. Later with development, education, and love it was hoped that the indigenous people ("the natives") would demand such a status.

This projection never became a reality. Frenchmen and Muslims who thought about it, doubted that it ever could. But in the time France held Algeria and served as protector in Tunisia and Morocco, many devoted servants tried to move in that direction. Muslim, Jew, and Frenchman alike took part in mutual experience. At the end, France ran down the tricolor and the Muslims assumed the responsibilities of independence in a mid-twentieth century world. The imprint of France could not immediately be erased, nor could the old Muslim civilization. To understand today's Maghrib, one must acquire a knowledge of both these influences and also familiarity with the international policies of the world after the second great war.

In Algeria, after 1830, various policies were tried by the French. These were often launched in an atmosphere of hostility, bordering upon active revolt. Abdelkader's resistance lasted for seventeen years after the conquest. Again in 1864, southern Oran province felt the uneasiness of revolt. In 1871 a particularly bitter insurrection broke out in Kabylia, while France was preoccupied with her own military disaster at the hands of Prussia. In 1954 the revolt which led directly to independence began. In a sense it can be considered as only one in a long list of uprisings, and the French regarded it as such in the beginning. But no one could really know the true feelings of the Muslims. Were the times of peaceful co-existence indicative of Algeria's state of mind, or were the sporadic and tenacious revolts?

In Algeria, the French experimented with many types of colonial administration, but none took permanent hold. In the early years after 1830, military occupation proceeded under a governor general whose orders came directly from the minister of war in Paris. Civil administrators aided the military. When the Second Republic replaced the Orléans monarchy in 1848, public services in Algeria fell under the control of the equivalent ministries in Paris, which meant that military rule declined. Departments and communes modeled after those of the Metropole took form. Early in the Second Empire, a minister of Algeria replaced the governor general, and prefects on the spot received larger responsibilities. General councils of Europeans functioned at the local level of government. By 1860, however, Napoleon III reestablished the office of governor general and increased the powers of the military, an opposite evolution from his program in France which moved from authoritarian toward democratic lines.

During the crisis of 1870, caused by occupation of northern France by the Prussian army, the Crémieux law granted French citizenship to the Jewish population of Algeria. The same privilege was theoretically extended to the Muslims, but since, in order to qualify they had to surrender their allegiance to Koranic statutes, few accepted. The Crémieux law tied the Jewish minority more firmly to the French colonials and made it a favored group.

The Third Republic found it difficult to decide where political power should actually reside in Algeria. This quandary meant that the authority of the governor general varied greatly. Sometimes the minister of interior in Paris held the reins tightly. At other periods, 1881 to 1896, for example, Algeria's government fell under the equivalent ministries in Paris, reducing the governor general to a figurehead. By the twentieth century, the governor general's power stood high and he was responsible to the French legislature.

All Muslims in Algeria were considered French "subjects." Those few who accepted French civil status and denied Islam received a "citizenship" which, theoretically at least, included the rights held by the Jewish population and the French. In 1903 when a Muslim became a Catholic convert and asked that he be admitted to full French citizenship, an Algiers court denied his claim. Muslims who became Catholics kept their legal status and did not become French.

Local Government

By 1919 assimilation reached the point where many Frenchmen viewed Algeria as an integral part of France. The governor general possessed wide powers, which he discharged upon the advice of a council of prominent European residents. By this time almost all Europeans in Algeria, regardless of their Spanish, Italian, or Mediterranean island origin, embraced French citizenship. Another advisory council, in which Muslims were represented, deliberated administrative questions. The Financial Delegations created in 1898, oversaw taxation and approved the budget. A Muslim minority sat in this important body.

Local government, where the state touched people's lives much more directly, was a complex structure. In the first instance, it stood directly divided between civil and military areas. The latter usually were isolated and sparsely inhabited by Europeans. In the back country of the Kabylia and Aurès mountains, the French imprint, to use an Arabic figure of speech, was little more than that a serpent makes while slithering over a rock. The people went their own ancient ways.

Three types of civil communes, the smallest unit of government, were current. "Full power" communes were modeled after those in France with an elected mayor and town council, both controlled down to the last detail by Europeans. "Mixed" communes differed in that they were administered by men appointed by the governor general. In these, a council of Europeans and Muslims helped reach decisions. Usually the "mixed" communes grouped several small villages. In military zones they fell under the control of an army officer. Finally, there were "native" communes in which a Muslim leader or caid ruled, aided by a council of notables (djemma), usually over the douar (Muslim community).

After 1871, Frenchmen from Algeria sat in the Chamber of Deputies. They busily waved the tricolor and blocked all efforts to improve the inferior status of the Muslims. These representatives looked upon Clemenceau as a traitor to France and French Algeria when, in 1919, he made a modest gesture of thanks for support rendered by the Muslims to France in 1914-1918. His extremely mild efforts to open French citizenship to a few Muslims and to increase their participation in local government brought a great protest, against which the "Tiger" stood firm.

This same colon lobby prevented the passage of the Blum-Violette bill in 1937. The bill provided that, in the first year of application, 21,000 elite Muslims would become full French citizens. When Muslim soldiers who had served France in distinguished fashion, teachers, and officials were denied access to the French nation, assimilation and French Algeria seemed a farce. But the French in Algeria waxed fat, well satisfied with the "maximum concessions" made in 1919.

In Morocco, French occupation moved more slowly than in Algeria and Tunisia and was less overpowering. The Sultan remained more than the theoretical fountainhead of power, and since the French protectorate dated from two years before the outbreak of World War I, it did not have time to consolidate the empire until 1920. France's great Resident General, Marshal Lyautey, found his major task to be pacification. Though he made great steps in the direction of bringing peace, the task was not completed until 1934, nine years after he left his post.

During World War I that intrepid French colonizer managed, with a skeleton force, to move forward with pacification. He defeated various tribal insurrections through a marvelously delicate combination of force and persuasion. With respect both for the Sultan and the Moroccan past, he refused to try to make Frenchmen of the people. Instead his idea was to lead the Moroccans into the twentieth century with a minimum of friction between European and Arabic ways. Thus the Europeans who came to work in Morocco lived separate lives, even as Lyautey worked to develop a trained indigenous elite, whom he envisaged might some day link Morocco directly to France.

The difficulty with this plan was that once the young Moroccans who were educated and exposed to the modern world were ready to take their places, Lyautey was gone. He had been replaced by a civilian chief whose military arm was Marshal Pétain. The Moroccan elite, unable to find responsible jobs, became a force of nationalist opposition to the French. In the Rif, Abdelkrim attacked the Spanish and then the French. By 1933 pacification may have been complete, but three years earlier the French-promulgated Berber *Dahir* (decree) was a direct contradiction of Lyautey's plan, for it tried to play off Berber against Arab. It stimulated Moroccan nationalist feeling. Thus, even before pacification was achieved, a new seed of rebellion had been planted.

The Problem of Viability

Whenever today's discussion turns to newly-independent countries in Africa or Asia, one of the most frequently raised questions is: Are these countries viable? Usually this question means, are the economies producing, will there be an increased living standard for the inhabitants? These questions were not asked by nationalists in the midst of planning strategy for independence campaigns. In the Maghrib, the nationalist goal of independence, while it might well imply a long-range economic and social betterment, focused upon political freedom which had a much more intimate relationship with status and pride than with immediate economic amelioration. Not to be known as a *"salarab"* (dirty Arab), to be at home in one's own country, to have equality before the law, to have absolutely equal opportunities for education, and even for literacy—these were the telling slogans of nationalist independence movements.

Still, the economic and social condition of Algeria, Tunisia, and Morocco before and after the French period are important questions in any discussion which seeks to understand those independent states. Usually in this consideration of economic and social institutions, two different interpretations are brought forth. Proud French spokesmen look at their work on the land and in the cities, cite French statistics, and ask the rhetorical question, where would these people be without us? The nationalist in Algeria, Tunisia, or Morocco on the eve of inde pendence raises a different question. "Who," he asks "owns the best land, who controls industry, who spends almost all the money, and who gets the education and the jobs?"

Many myths color the picture which the casual visitor to the Maghrib or the average reader carries in his mind. The European population was never solely composed of exploiters who came to make money. Most of them were ordinary people with a little more capacity for adventure and hard work than most. They had little savings upon arrival, and tried to build in the colony or protectorate a better life than they were likely to have at home. Public servants and administrators carried out the orders of superiors. There were, particularly in Tunisia, a large number of these—too many, thought the Tunisians. In Morocco a long struggle was invested to achieve order and financial stability for the state.

Nor, by the same token, were all (or many) Muslims violent terrorists who loved to cut European throats. Most of them were humble, poor people who tried to gain a life from the soil. The events attending the transition from colony to independence were scarcely more violent in Tunisia and Morocco than happenings of ordinary years. In Algeria a considerable amount of violence prevailed in the mountainous areas (where European influence was small) almost continuously from 1830 to November 1, 1954, the day the crucial rebellion began.

We shall never really know what these areas would have done, what the people would have become, if the Europeans had not come in the nineteenth century. No controlled experiments in behavioral science are possible on this scale. If the Europeans had not come, some other peoples might have. Or perhaps a great Arab renaissance could have evolved. Possibly the tribal culture would have gone its own way and tried to solve social problems in traditional fashion, without benefit of Western science, technology, and nationalism. In this case those people might have considered themselves more viable, by their standards, than they did during the European occupation. Viability can be a relative matter.

What did happen, was that Europeans entered Northwest Africa, bringing with them Western institutions. They imposed these standards, and the indigenous culture could not resist them. By the twentieth century, when the nationalist-independence movements began to be influential, many of the inhabitants of the Maghrib stood in a cultural no man's land, somewhere between the traditional culture and the new one introduced by the Europeans.

In Algeria (where the French occupation lasted 124 years before the outbreak of the rebellion which led to independence), reliable data explain fairly clearly what happened, even if they do not guarantee a single or simple interpretation.

Land-Holding and Agriculture

Take the basic question of land-holding and agriculture, the productive heart of the Algerian economy. In 1841 General Bugeaud gave the following advice: "Wherever the water supply is good and the land fertile, there we must place colonists without worrying about previous owners. We must distribute the lands in full title to the colonists." [1] By a law of November 1, 1844, French authorities incorporated, as French public domain, all lands on which there were no buildings (unimproved land) when Muslim proprietors could not justify holding title before the 1830 French conquest. This law, either intended a massive expropriation or showed an extremely deep ignorance of Islamic law as well as Berber family and tribal practice.

> The bond which united the fellah to his land is mystical rather than utilitarian. He belongs to his fields much more than his fields belong to him. He is attached to his land by deeply affective ties as witness the agrarian rites in which is expressed a sentiment of dependency in regard to this land, which cannot be treated as a mere raw material but rather as a foster-mother whose authority must be obeyed, since, in the final analysis, it is on her benevolence or ill-will, much more than on human effort, that wealth or poverty depend . . .
>
> The land is an end in itself and not a mere means of existence, and work is not a way of earning a living but a way of life. With this in mind, the following often noted characteristic of the precapitalist spirit may perhaps be better understood: an increase in wages brings about a reduction in the amount of work performed.[2]

[1] Quoted by Alain Savary, Nationalisme algérien et grandeur française (Paris: Plon, 1960), p. 27.

[2] Pierre Bourdieu, The Algerians (Boston: Beacon Press, 1962), pp. 103-104; the English translation of Sociologie de l'Algérie (Paris: Presses Universitaires de France, 1958).

An 1845 ordinance allowed French military authorities to sequester the holdings of Muslims guilty of "hostile acts." The imposition of European rules by force upon an Islamic community deprived Muslims of their land and garnered French public domain which was used as bait to attract colonists. All kinds of people came to Algeria. Retired soldiers stayed on; speculators sent over the gullible; political opponents of Louis Napoleon's coup d'état of December 2, 1851, landed in Algeria; refugees from Alsace-Lorraine arrived in 1871; felons went there to get a fresh start; and, of course, farmers, businessmen, and civil servants came too. Land policy varied, but usually terms were made attractive to colonists. France needed settlers to hold the colony and to make it profitable.

Before the revolution of 1954, Europeans owned approximately one-third of the cultivable land and nearly all the best land. The average European holding amounted to roughly 124 hectares,* compared to the Muslim holding of 11 hectares, according to one source, an 11 to 1 ratio. A French official source published in 1955 placed the ratio at 17 to 1 in favor of the Europeans.

The Europeans owned the best land and they exploited it by modern methods. They occupied the moist coastal areas, benefiting from government support on price, credit, improvements, and protection. Muslim farmers gravitated to less productive marginal land where they used the old primitive methods of agriculture under a patriarchal system. By the end of the French period, half the agricultural output found its way into European pockets; yet 97 per cent of the rural population were Muslims. Many were forced to earn wages on European-owned land or to go to France to work. Increasingly the expanding Muslim population moved toward pauperization. This led nationalist spokesmen to argue that the choice was between starvation and rebellion.

Actually, the French vastly increased the amount of producing land, from roughly 1,400,000 acres in 1830 when the population was perhaps 2,000,000 persons, to 7,000,000 acres in 1954 when 10,000,000 people lived in Algeria. Areas such as the Mitidja plain near Algiers, which had been swampy and malarial, were transformed by the French into fertile plantations.

* One hectare = 2.47 acres.

Several points stand out as warning signals. Food production failed to keep pace with population increase. Two systems of agriculture, one modern, the other primitive, existed side by side. There was small opportunity for evolution of the primitive system, which was based upon a different concept of land's function. The owners lacked the capital and training to change even if they so desired. When independence came, European owners found conditions imposed which resembled those of their own land conquest in the years following 1830. Just as the great mosque of Algiers became a cathedral and then, in 1962, once again a mosque, so the land which the Muslims lost in 1831 returned to the hands of their descendants or to the state.

Industrialization and Modernization

To read the official accounts of French industrial achievement, is to understand why the French took pride in their work. By 1954, Algerian mines yielded important quantities of iron, phosphates, lead, zinc, antimony, and copper. Two years later the first oil flowed from a large estimated reserve in the Sahara, and an important quantity of natural gas lay waiting exploitation. These basic products could be transported on 50,000 miles of good roads, almost 19,000 miles of highways, or 3,000 miles of railroad track, to modern ports in Algiers, Oran, and Bône where efficient ships carried them to the world. Coal from the Kenadsa fields in southern Oranais supplied 20 per cent of Algeria's needs, and power stations generated large quantities of electricity. A modest industrialization, which did not seriously compete with French output, took shape.

Compared to the almost nonexistent economic activity of 1830, these accomplishments cannot be ignored. By 1954 Algeria's trade volume reached $1,023,000,000 with imports amounting to $623,-000,000 and exports reaching $400,000,000. The Customs Union between Algeria and Metropolitan France accounted for 79 per cent of exports. A trade deficit of $223,000,000 resulted (according to French economists) from the determined effort to raise living standards by importing machinery and capital goods.

It is a reasonable assumption that Algerian industry in 1830, apart from hand-craft products such as rugs, embroidery, brass, and leather work was nil. France herself, in 1830, presented a marked contrast to today's powerful plant. Surely the mother country developed itself more purposefully than it did the colony. This was common practice among the European imperial powers. Invariably, too, European businessmen who went into the colonies sought to make money—this was natural. Nevertheless, in 1954, intelligent Algerians rankled that 90 per cent of industry and the profits of industry and agriculture fell into European hands, although they knew this situation related in direct proportion to investment and training.

Before the Muslims could participate more profitably in the economic and political life of Algeria, they were advised to get an education or to learn a trade. For a long period many resisted this advice. Before 1939 few Muslims sent their children to French schools. Still, by 1954, some half-million European and Muslim children attended French schools which were financed by 17 per cent of the ordinary budget for Algeria.

Yet the fact that in 1954 some 94 per cent of the Muslim males and 90 per cent of the females remained illiterate in French glaringly exposed an inadequate educational program. The University of Algiers, with a faculty of nearly one hundred professors and an enrollment of 5,000 students, ranked as a strong institution. Four-fifths of the students were Europeans. Perhaps 150,000 young Muslims attended the traditional Koranic schools which emphasized Arabic civilization, rather than European.

Another less formal school to which the increasing numbers of Algerian men gravitated in the decade after 1945, was the Metropolitan French labor market. By 1954 a half-million Algerians worked in France. Usually they arrived with little or no knowledge of the language, and no training. Their hope was to learn a trade, send money home to their families, and eventually to return to Algeria. In France they faced a brutal experience. Unskilled, they willingly accepted the heaviest, most disagreeable work. Often they lived so badly in the damp cold of the north, that they undermined their already precarious health. From this experience, however, arose the largest pool of skilled and semi-skilled Algerian workers.

This experience (which, due to rotation, possibly involved two million men over a short period of time) also produced a divergence of reaction. Some returned home bent upon making Algeria a modern, independent country. Others remained in France working for one or another of the new Algerian political parties. French trade unions captured some and so did the French Communist Party. All became familiar with a new world, a place where many resolved to play a new part. A few gained higher educational opportunities in the Metropole, and these young men formed student organizations dedicated to bettering the lot of Muslims in Algeria. A small number fit their lives into the European pattern and became truly French.

A survey of nonagricultural employment in Algeria in 1954 indicates that some Muslims were beginning to hold positions of responsibility. This evolution came too late to prevent rebellion. By the year of the rebellion, 90 per cent of the unemployed in Algeria were Muslims. Seven per cent of "civil servants and intellectuals" and 95 per cent of the day laborers were Muslims. Estimates showed seventeen out of one hundred "lower level intellectuals and technicians" to be Muslim. And the overwhelmingly majority of the Muslim population cultivated the land either primitively for themselves or as day laborers for the Europeans.[3]

In Morocco, agricultural output compared favorably with Algeria as late as 1910. After 1912 the French systematically obtained some of the best land in Morocco. Of the 11,000,000 acres under cultivation in 1950 approximately 2,500,000 were owned by six to seven thousand French; 850,000 Moroccans held the remainder. Two thirds of the French landowners bought it themselves, while one third acquired allotments, between 1918-1935, of requisitioned land. Lyautey's description of land policy in 1916 resembled Bugeaud's advice in Algeria in 1841. "The French legation was induced to encourage a horde of Frenchmen to stake out land and take possession, creating titles to this land without inquiring too closely into their legal rights to it."[4]

Before 1912 Morocco exported cereals and other foodstuffs, but after 1940 when agricultural output fell behind population growth, cereals had to be imported. Fresh vegetables, linseed oil, sugar, olives, and citrus fruits were shipped abroad and usually some 4,000,000 U.S. gallons of wine reached France. By 1950 a thriving canned herring

---

[3] Savary, pp. 18-19.
[4] Quoted by Pierre Parent, *Causeries sur le Maroc de 1951* (Toulouse, Imprimerie Régionale, 1951), p. 8.

industry packed 35,000 metric tons. Livestock played an important part in economic life, and in the twenty-five year period 1925-1949 sheep production rose 50 per cent. Goats doubled in numbers, and increases among cattle, donkeys, camels, mules, and pigs were steady. The French reclaimed a million acres of land through dam construction, and a reforestation effort greatly benefited the economy and the land.

Morocco's mineral resources, long an important national asset, underwent intensive exploitation after World War II. This process accelerated when the Korean War further increased demand. Phosphate production fell under the control of the *Office Cherifien des Phosphates* created in 1920; other minerals were mined by private companies. By 1955, phosphates, lead, and manganese (important in hardening steel), were the major mineral exports.

Before 1921 no modern Moroccan industry existed. Skilled artisans had for centuries produced leather goods, carpets, mosaics, pottery (faïence), and certain textiles. However, because these artisans had a hard time adapting themselves to modern industrial methods, French workers usually filled the better jobs in the industrial labor market. Moroccan artisans preferred to remain in their regular habitat, working with hand tools. They did not wish to face the urban labor market or the attendant housing problem, which often meant living in a *bidonville*—a hovel built of discarded petrol cans, wood, and rags. Nevertheless, many Moroccan workers, mostly untrained for modern industrial operations, gravitated to the cities. By 1950, Casablanca had five *bidonville* quarters, the largest housing 60,000 persons.

In that year the schools educated 64,000 European, 120,000 Muslim, and 32,000 Jewish youth. Perhaps another 13,000 pupils attended itinerant schools. Since there were 2,000,000 youth of school age, this meant that 6-7 per cent of the young Moroccans went to school. Most of the teachers were French. No more than 22 Moroccans ranked as qualified teachers (*cadre général*), although 240 high school graduates taught without any teacher training.

As in Algeria, the French developed a modern transportation system. By 1951 they had laid 1100 miles of railroad track, one third of which accommodated electric powered trains. 27,000 miles of road, a quarter of which could be used in all seasons, connected various areas. The modern port of Casablanca, which handled 6,000,000 tons of freight, was another lasting French creation.

Until the Korean War, Morocco often suffered a trade deficit. In 1950, imports exceeded exports by 5 billion old francs (roughly $10,-000,000). France took 60 per cent of goods sent abroad, and furnished 68 per cent of imports. State revenue came from the *tertib* (tax on land), plus taxes on industry, commerce, and such state monopolies as tobacco and postal services. The largest Moroccan expenditure in 1950—the last good base year because of increasing political tensions between Moroccan nationalists and France—was for administration. These costs amounted to 36 per cent of total expenditure.

Modernization and economic development required trained civil servants, who were French, in overwhelming numbers. Moroccan spokesmen insisted that their country supported an overabundance of administrators whose numbers, between 1938 and 1950, rose from 19,145 to 41,450.[5]

Of the three Northwest African French dependencies, Tunisia was "the smallest, the most tranquil," and unfortunately, the poorest in natural resources. One of the first major changes made by the French administration was the installation of French legal forms as a system for Europeans parallel to Islamic law, which applied to Muslims. The capitulations allowing consular tribunals for foreigners, extended earlier by the Bey to various European countries (except Italy), were withdrawn. By 1896 Italy finally renounced its capitulation. This meant that Europeans came under the jurisdiction of French justice.

The Bey recognized that Islamic law which, for example, prohibited interest-bearing loans, was incompatible with modern economic requirements. As a result, Beylical decrees supported the French code as it related to corporation law, commercial regulations, contracts, patents, and all major aspects of the law of commerce.

In a country where agriculture was traditionally the predominant economic activity, the future well-being of the people depended upon land and yield improvement. Any program to increase productivity was complicated by the three prevalent systems of land tenure: *melk*

---

[5] Many of the facts and figures employed in the above discussion of Morocco have been taken from Rom Landau, "Morocco," *International Conciliation*, no. 483 (September 1952), pp. 311-360.

(freehold); *habous* (religious endowments); and "collective" or tribal lands. The *habous*, managed by descendants of the donor as private lands, or by the state as public lands, reduced a vast acreage to the status of mortmain. Land transfers were not published and the uncertainty of titles and deeds added another burden to the reform program.

Under the prodding of the protectorate, the Bey cooperated with the French to produce a common law regime, and Koranic and customary practices were altered by legislation. At the same time, a Topographical Service cooperating with a Mixed Land Tribunal registered and cleared titles to two million hectares. By 1885 a code based upon French, German, and Australian (the Torrens Act) precedents clearly defined procedure.

This change favored European colonists by encouraging capital investment. Later legislation, however, protected small landowners against speculation and allowed the peasant who worked *habous* and tribal lands the opportunity of acquiring title. The process of transferring *habous* and tribal lands to individual holders was still far from complete when Tunisia gained independence in 1956. Some "semi-official" distribution of tribal lands to members also took place. Europeans held approximately 26 per cent of the land under cultivation when the protectorate ended in 1956, most of it in the fertile Tell (hilly area stretching inland from the coast). On the average, French farms ran 750 acres, while Italian holdings were one-tenth that size.

Two unique agricultural contracts bear mentioning. The *enzel* allowed the acquisition of the property of a trust (such as a *habous*) by a payment of perpetual annual rent. The *mgharsa*, or planting lease, allowed a person who planted fruit trees (usually olives) to receive half the tended land in freehold from the owner.

Many improvements in agriculture took place during the protectorate. Scientific advice, machinery, low-interest loans, and producer cooperatives all came to Tunisia. Heavy investments were made to aid the *fellahin* (peasant) and to improve the agriculture of the parched central and southern zones. The greatest obstacle was the lack of water. Fortunately, determined efforts to trap and retain this bounty, which included drilling Artesian wells, constructing dams, and reforestation programs, yielded excellent results.

Cereals could, in good years, be exported: usually some 40 per cent of agricultural income came from them. The entire Esparto grass crop was bought by Britain, until a Tunisian paper pulp factory demanded this raw material. Tunisian wines, produced by French and Italian families, sold well in the domestic market and were exported. Citrus fruit and vegetables found a ready market on the other side of the Mediterranean. Somewhere between 23 and 26 million olive trees yielded a variable quantity of olive oil (depending upon rainfall), and many tons of dates reached the market place each year.

Cultivation of livestock has, in recent years, amounted to approximately 20 per cent of agricultural income. Sheep, goats, and cattle provided the mainstay, but horses, mules, asses, camels, and pigs were also raised. This industry, so dependent upon rainfall and proper pasturage, was often subject to sharp fluctuation. The drought in 1961 reduced sheep production so violently that prices increased fivefold. Fortunately, the coastal waters provide a rich variety of fish which are brought in by some 15,000 fishermen. In general, fish is excellent in the coastal cities, where the meat is unreliable.

Modern Tunisian industry has suffered from the shortage of energy-providing fuels. Almost no coal or oil has been discovered. Hydroelectric power requires water and dams, and while this energy source received attention during the later years of the protectorate, total output fell short of requirements. Imported coal and oil have traditionally filled the gap.

Phosphates, iron, lead, and zinc are in good supply. The quality of the Tunisian phosphate deposits is below that mined in Morocco, but through processing, super-phosphates are produced and sold in large amounts—10 per cent of world consumption in 1955. Iron ore, lead, and zinc are important exports, but demand (and price) depend upon the world production-consumption situation. Tunisia also exports salt and cement. Home processing industries include fruit and fish canning, flour, semolina, macaroni, and tobacco.

With a population explosion, which in recent times has increased 25 per cent each decade, Tunisia required a steady increase in the rhythm of agricultural and industrial production to stay even. French assistance, through various heavy subsidies and loans, maintained living standards despite a drop in per capita production. However, with death rates down, birth rates up, and increased longevity easily outdistancing the making of goods and food in recent decades, independent Tunisia faced a serious challenge. A French source, issued at the moment of independence, emphasized the special nature of "a country which, largely helped from [the] outside up to now, has perhaps been prevented from fully realizing its true situation." [6]

MUSLIM POPULATION INCREASE IN TUNISIA[7]

| | Muslim Population | | Increase per Decade | |
Period	Beginning of Period	End of Period	Numerical	Percentage
1881-1911	1,500,000	1,740,000	80,000	5%
1911-1921	1,740,000	1,890,000	150,000	9%
1921-1931	1,890,000	2,160,000	270,000	14%
1926-1936	1,930,000	2,340,000	410,000	21%
1936-1946	2,340,000	2,920,000	580,000	25%

Possibly the most striking accomplishment of the French protectorate, particularly during the decade after 1945, was the expansion of educational facilities. With a trained population, many hitherto impossible problems could at least be faced. Productivity might be made to keep pace with population increase; and as a larger fraction became educated and oriented toward the modern world, it was possible that population growth itself would level off. During the last years of the protectorate, one-third of the ordinary state budget flowed into education. Between 1945-1955 classrooms increased by nearly 50 per cent.

SCHOOL ATTENDANCE IN TUNISIA[8]

| | School Attendance | | Number of Pupils per 1,000 Inhabitants | |
Period	Total	Muslims	Total Population	Muslim Population
1883	3,000	1,000	2	0.6
1911	40,000	12,000	20	18
1936	92,000	43,000	35	18
1954	265,000	212,000	74	60

[6] "Tunisia Faces the Future," *Le Monde Économique* (June 1, 1960), 109.
[7] This chart from *ibid.*, 107.
[8] Chart from *ibid.*, 99.

As in Algeria and Morocco the French administration built a strong, serviceable transport system, including approximately 6,000 miles of road and 1300 miles of railroad. The ports of Tunis and La Goulette were adapted in order to receive and handle ocean-going ships.

The Gallic imprint clearly altered the land and the people of the Maghrib. A relatively small minority of Frenchmen (larger in Algeria) ran the government. local administration, and most economic activity. The French also invested most of the capital and took the profits. Their influence was always greatest along the coast and the Tell area. Berber and Arab never relinquished the back country or the desert.

Although a colon spirit evolved in the French and European communities of the three areas, in Algeria, where occupation began nearly a century earlier than Morocco, and where the political regime of the Turks and the Dey were wiped out, it dominated both thought and action: "Algeria was French; my grandfather came here and carved this farm from a wilderness." French institutions in Tunisia and Morocco were tempered by the presence of the Bey and Sultan and the pre-existing customs. In Algeria few checks and balances impeded direct French administration. Nor was there ever a serious attempt to apply an honest policy of assimilation beyond the expediency of a protectorate. In all three areas a European superstructure, or façade, evolved upon an Arabo-Berber base. Between the two, war and peace, intransigency and compromise, hate and love, loyalty and treachery prevailed. Power rested in French hands, but the people belonged to themselves, an unknown quantity.

FIVE

Tunisian Nationalism

Before 1952

Origins of Anti-Colonialism

"The expedition into Tunisia which marked the resumption of French expansion, and which gave birth to the colonial talents of Ferry,* also began the tradition of an aggressive anti-colonialism which was never completely disarmed."[1] Thus Jean Ganiage, the distinguished French student of the origins of the protectorate of 1881, recognized that, from the beginning, French influence faced the challenge of indigenous Tunisian forces. One may call them anti-colonialist, anti-Western, anti-French, or finally, Tunisian nationalist. They existed from the beginning of the French period, becoming increasingly strong, and ultimately, in 1956, leading to independence.

Anti-colonial forces came from Paris, where Tunisian students were steeped in French egalitarian thought, and from the eastern Mediterranean, where Arab spokesmen pressed for a Muslim renascence. By 1939, Tunisian youth had also been exposed to ideas of self-determination and a mandate system under international (League of Nations) supervision.

As early as 1907 "Young Tunisians," led by students who had been

* French premier in 1881 who directed negotiations leading to the protectorate in Tunis. An ardent imperialist, he later pressed French expansion on Madagascar, the Congo, Niger, and Indo-China.

[1] Jean Ganiage, Les origines du protectorate français en Tunisie 1861-1881 (Paris: Presses Universitaires de France, 1951), p. 699.

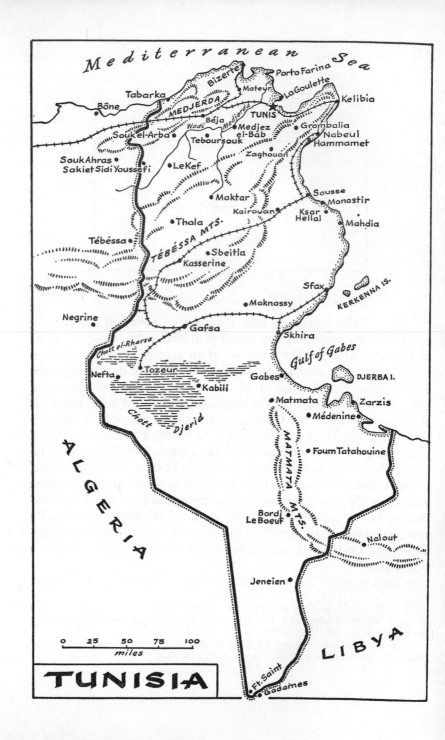

taught the whole range of French thought, chose the egalitarian-republican rather than the "elitist" authoritarian line then being furthered by groups like *Action Française*. To improve the condition of the Muslim, they advocated modernization through newspapers and self-improvement societies. To meet the challenges of the twentieth century through the study of the Young Turks was the stated purpose of Muslim reformers such as Mohammed Abdou.

Some Eastern prophets concerned themselves seriously with the idea of recreating a united Islamic state which would span the Mediterranean south shore from the Near East to Ceuta. Culturally this pan-Islamic view had merit; practically, under twentieth-century conditions, it overshot the target. No united Islamic or Arabic state took shape. Still, in seeking to adapt Koranic teachings, where state and church were fused, these myth-makers raised important questions for would-be nationalists in the Maghrib. But, for the time being, the two lines of reform fixed upon a common goal—the emancipation of the Tunisian branch of the Arab world.

The French administration, in the process of making its rule increasingly direct, efficient, and productive (particularly for its nationals), resisted these anti-colonial forces. To have joined them, it thought, would have opened the road to Tunisian independence. The opposite course ultimately led to the same result. Relatively speaking, though force and Tunisian counterforce were used, Tunisian nationalist aspiration fulfilled itself against the French administration without recourse to general violence.

Incidents, such as the one at the Muslim cemetery at Dzellaz in 1911, where the French tried to transfer this hallowed Muslim ground to the European orbit, led to fighting and to the exile of Tunisian leaders. Before the end of World War I, Young Tunisians exercised important influence, but had really failed to touch the older generation. The war and the peace-making encouraged the view that colonial claims should be adjusted in the interests of the populations concerned. "Self-determination," that magic word which never applied to the Northwest African French empire, lost none of its appeal to the alert Young Tunisians. And in 1919 the French again involved themselves in a religio-economic incident which brought the older generation to the Young Tunisians' doorstep.

The French tried to transfer large sections of *habous* lands from the traditional Muslim religious groups to European farmers. This attempt offended the "Old Turbans" (Tunisians who had no objection to French presence as long as Muslim institutions, particularly religious, were respected). As a result, they joined the Young Tunisians whose modernism they had earlier questioned. France, seeking to pursue its colonial economic aims and to recover from the frightful losses sustained in the First World War, fused the new and the old Tunisia against herself.

In 1920 Tunisia's first political party, the *Destour* (Constitution) took form under the leadership of Cheikh Taalbi. Its name harked back to the constitution of 1857, promulgated by the Bey for a short time after a revolt. As a precedent, it loomed ominously for the French because it contained a guarantee of fundamental rights and legal equality despite condition of race or religion. In 1920, Destour's program called for freedom of the Tunisian people and a constitution by which they would elect an Assembly and sit in it along with French representatives. Other basic freedoms (press and assembly), plus opportunity for Tunisians to serve in government posts, were also asserted.

Although France opposed such a program, the protectorate did react to this prodding in 1923 by opening the gates of French citizenship to qualified Tunisians. The condition that this elite live under French, instead of Islamic, law mean that few accepted. Religious leaders fulminated against the French denial of Islamic culture. The nationalists had gone too far to accept this gesture, which applied to only one per cent of the nation. Taalbi and other Destour leaders were exiled and the party went underground. Demonstrations and boycotts continued and, in 1933, another cemetery incident—this time at Monastir—led to renewed violence.

The Destour party made no striking forays in defense of the nationalist interest in the 1920's. A much more important evolution was taking place in the lives of young Tunisians studying at home and abroad. They were keenly aware of the changing world and they awaited the day when, with France, they would lead their country toward new goals. One of these young men was Habib Bourguiba, born in 1903 in Monastir, the youngest of eight children. By 1919 he interrupted his studies to recuperate from pneumonia in Le Kef, where his brother ran a hospital. Later in Tunis, at French Lycée Carnot, he hovered on the fringes of the Destour. Then in Paris he achieved degrees in law and political science. Not only did he develop a respect for the free environment that was student Paris in the mid-1920's, he also married a French girl. Loving France but hating colonialism, he returned to Tunis in 1927.

Immediately he became involved in Destour, whose newspaper, *La Voix du Tunisien,* he helped edit. In his circle—including his brother Mohammed and Dr. Mohammed Materi, Tahar Sfar, and the younger Salah ben Youssef—he pushed for greater activity, for more than anti-colonial utterance. This group sharpened party organization into a potent weapon which recruited support throughout the population. In 1932 they published *L'Action Tunisienne,* a newspaper that sought to open communication between French and Tunisian minds and, by examining the crisis of Tunisian life, to educate and recruit the masses. By 1934 the Destour old guard, realizing that these younger men were seizing party control by direct appeal to the nation, tried a power play in the party congress. When it failed, Bourguiba's group founded the Neo-Destour, in which he served as secretary general under President Materi.

Bourguiba and Neo-Destour

Bourguiba proved to be much more than an apt phrase-maker (although this ability was itself of incalculable value). The man who could define independence, the Neo-Destour's basic objective, as "human dignity translated into political terms," knew how to pluck the heart strings and, at the same time, appeal to one of Western civilization's proudest legacies. Nor was he the bomb-throwing kind of nationalist leader, a twentieth-century Mazzini imploring his followers to charge the machine guns. He knew that France must in the long run agree to Tunisian independence. He also knew that it could not be won by Tunisian force alone.

The Neo-Destour, therefore, followed an evolutionary nationalist approach—first a voice in the protectorate, then autonomy, finally independence. This "Fabian nationalism" [2] focused first upon winning the battle of colonialism in the hearts of the Tunisians themselves.

To do this, a "going to the country" movement was organized. Reminiscent of the Populists in nineteenth-century Russia, the Neo-Destour sent intellectuals and students into the remote villages to instruct the population. Not simply teaching literacy, but also explaining the necessity of relating Islam to modern needs, these battalions worked for independence at the grass roots. One of the Neo-Destour's early convictions, carried into independent Tunisia after 1956, was that traditional religious practices such as asceticism, Ramadan fasting, and useless demonstrating, should be abandoned. Neo-Destour concerned itself with politics and avoided religious fanaticism. This posture enabled many Jews to enroll in the party without pangs of conscience.

Party structure closely resembled that of the Communist party, though its ideology was entirely different. Basic cells formed regional federations which elected members to a national congress which, in turn, named a political bureau of twelve. The party represented a cross-section, a fair sample of the Tunisian people of all classes and occupations. The goal of an independent Tunisia attracted all classes and, although the party was monolithic in structure, wide opinions were debated. Neither French, international, nor Tunisian communists ever obtained serious influence in the party or the independent state.

The immediate success of the Neo-Destour can be gauged from the intense repression it called forth from the French administration, and the fierce and undying opposition of the colons. Late in 1934, Resident General Peyrouton jailed its leaders and banned all meetings. When Bourguiba and the other leaders like Ben Youssef were jailed, new men, such as the brilliant Mongi Slim, whose family had come from Greece with the Turks, the economist Hedi Nouira, and Ali Belhouane, the Arabic scholar, replaced them, and the party stood firm.

[2] The phrase is Lorna Hahn's. See her excellent analysis *North Africa: Nationalism to Nationhood* (Washington: Public Affairs Press, 1960), p. 18 and *passim*.

Momentarily, the Popular Front* under Léon Blum in Paris relaxed the repressive measures and allowed a dialogue with the Tunisian leaders. Short-lived promises that Tunisians could play a more active role in government foundered upon the opposition of the colons, whose lobby in Paris succeeded in reinstalling an iron-fisted French administration in Tunisia. On April 10, 1937, a huge but peaceful Tunisian protest demonstration, ordered by Bourguiba, drew French fire. Some two hundred Tunisians were killed. This was followed by the arrest of three thousand members of the party, including Bourguiba and, later, Ladgham.

The Impact of World War II

When war struck Europe in September 1939, the Neo-Destour leaders were still in prison and the party, though not crushed, had been driven underground. Before France collapsed under the German juggernaut, Bourguiba almost faced a French firing squad. This close call for the Tunisian leader came about when French military authorities accepted as true a forged Italian charge that Bourguiba had engaged in espionage for Italy. A stay of execution ordered by the French resident general allowed time to disprove the incriminating document. By May 1940, when France reeled under the *Wehrmacht's* assault, Premier Paul Reynaud and war minister Daladier tried to buy Italian neutrality with an offer of Franco-Italian condominium in Tunisia. Mussolini, riding high on the wave of Hitler's victories over France, refused because he expected to gain all of Tunisia for Italy. This offer, which violated France's obligations to Tunisia under the Bardo and La Marsa protectorate, was purely a desperation measure.[3]

The Neo-Destour shrewdly understood its best interests, even though caught between occupied France and the imperialism of Italy and Nazi Germany. Its leaders, transferred from Tunisian to French prisons, where they remained until November 18, 1942, understood

---

* French elections in April-May, 1936, strengthened the parties of the left. As a result the *Rassemblement Populaire* (Popular Front), which campaigned under the slogan "freedom, work, bread, and peace," came to power under Blum. His cabinet was composed of Socialists and Radicals. The Communists, who won 72 votes, supported the government but refused to sit in the cabinet.

[3] Hahn, pp. 23-24.

that no advantage could be gained from changing imperial masters in the midst of an undecided war. Sympathy lay with the French. From his prison, Bourguiba passed the word to his wife and son, who visited him in August 1942, that Germany would be crushed. "Tunisia must work with the democracies to the fullest. . . . We can discuss independence after the war has been won." [4]

The Vichy French administration's anxiety to keep the French empire intact, first led to a conciliatory policy in Tunisia. The new Bey, Sidi-Mohammed al Moncef (known as Moncef Bey), pressed his advantage by forming a national ministry in December 1942. This ministry included Mohammed Chenik, vice-president of the Grand Council, Doctor Materi, the Neo-Destour veteran, Salah Ferhat, a member of the old Destour, and two non-nationalists, Mustapha Kaak and Abdelaziz Djellouli. This bold step toward reasserting Tunisian control of the government was possible largely because the German occupation of eastern Tunisia, the previous month, forced the Vichy Resident General to cooperate with the people. For the moment, colon influence fell to nil. The German presence forced the French to open the jail doors, to remove censorship rules, and to allow assemblies. Not since the Popular Front had Tunisia seen so much liberty, equality, and fraternity.

On November 8, 1942, another element entered Northwest Africa. The Anglo-American invasion "Operation Torch" landed large numbers of well-equipped fighting men at Casablanca, Oran, Algiers, Bougie, Djidjelli, and Bône. Much hard fighting lay ahead before these forces, cooperating with the British Eighth Army (which was driving westward from Egypt), destroyed the Axis army in May 1943, in Tunisia.[5]

The full impact of the Anglo-American victory upon the Northwest African people remains to be measured. It is certain that French prestige was lowered another notch, even though French political authority returned with the Anglo-American armies. The countries which wrote the Atlantic Charter wiped out the Italo-German invasion. Would they apply that charter, which promised a guarantee of

[4] Hahn, p. 25.
[5] Dwight D. Eisenhower, *Crusade in Europe* (New York: Doubleday, 1948), pp. 95-134.

the right of people to choose their form of government? What did a statement like "no territorial changes which do not accord with the wishes of the people's concerned" mean for the peoples of Tunisia, Morocco, and Algeria? Were those lines addressed to the colons or to the vast majority—the Muslims?

Upon seven members of the political bureau of the Neo-Destour, including Bourguiba, who sat in various French prisons, "Operation Torch" had an important result. The prisoners were picked up by the Germans at Chalon-sur-Saône and sent to Rome, where Bourguiba was luxuriously installed in the Piacentini Palace. The asking price for this splendor was, of course, collaboration. Bourguiba blithely demanded Tunisian independence, something the Axis might write on a paper but could not deliver in the face of Count Ciano's 1938 cry for "Tunisia, Djibouti, and Corsica." On April 8, 1943, five years after his imprisonment, Bourguiba returned to Tunis, to continue the work for independence.

Postwar Evolution

When the Anglo-American armies entered that city a month later, Bourguiba pledged support to France and the Allies for an ultimate victory. "The entire French nation, once liberated from the Nazi yoke, will not forget . . . its true friends, those whom she will have found at her side during these difficult times. . . ." This appeal fell on deaf official French ears. Much had changed since French officialdom with its paper army shook in its boots when the German army moved into Tunisia. France had been rescued and the United States had assured prostrate France six days before the "Torch" landings that her sovereignty "should be re-established as soon as possible over all territories, Metropolitan as well as colonial, over which the French flag waved in 1939." [6]

French authorities in Tunisia could afford to revert to the policy of repression. General Alphonse Juin, acting Resident General, and General Giraud saw to it that Bourguiba's statement "For a Franco-Tunisian Bloc" was quashed, because they feared Tunisian nationalism might make too many friends. Juin went much further; he accused

---

[6] William L. Langer, *Our Vichy Gamble* (New York: Knopf, 1947), p. 333, quoting "Murphy to Giraud," November 2, 1942, in OSS files.

Bourguiba of treason. American Consul General Hooker Doolittle protected the Tunisian and may well have saved his life. Moncef Bey, the outspoken ruler of Tunisia was the next target and, accused of collaboration with the Nazis, was interned in southern Algeria. That this conduct blatantly violated the La Marsa treaty (by which the French presence protected, rather than disposed of, the Bey), made no difference. Moncef Bey died in exile in 1947.

In 1943 and 1944 the French administrative grip tightened gradually. The powers of the Resident General increased at the expense of Tunisian participation in government, dashing the hopes of Neo-Destour leaders that, once the war returned to Europe from North Africa and the Allies had won, France would be generous to nationalist aspiration. France, however, had lost too much self-esteem to behave generously toward others. Its leaders faced not simply the gigantic task of explaining the debacle of 1940 and the attending moral collapse, but also the more pressing task of trying to reconstruct the sadly tarnished republic. This forced the Neo-Destour to adopt new tactics.

Since the party's objective development toward independence in peaceful cooperation with France did not seem possible, a decision was taken to assert the cause abroad. At the same time Neo-Destour strengthened itself at home, so that it could lead the nation, no matter what the future held.

Late in March 1945, some five weeks before Nazi Germany surrendered to the Allies, Bourguiba left Tunisia for Cairo, where he sought the support of the Arab Near East. Cairo at least provided a platform from which he could freely speak to the world. In articles and public addresses he highlighted the importance of Northwest Africa in the forthcoming power struggle between the West and the Soviet Communist world. At the same time he showed a more serious concern for the independence aspirations of Morocco and Algeria. From Cairo, too, he bitterly criticized French practices in the Maghrib, comparing the protector's colonial posture unfavorably with that of the British.

After visiting several countries, Bourguiba turned up in New York, late in 1946, to plead Tunisia's case before the United Nations delegations. In Washington he met unofficially various American Middle

East specialists. Nothing concrete resulted; he simply met and talked, hoping to make the world aware of his people's hopes. He soon returned to Cairo where, with other leaders, such as the Moroccan Al-Fassi, he helped create the Maghrib Office in 1947. In September 1949 Bourguiba returned to Tunisia convinced that external fence-mending, while profitable, could only supplement a direct dialogue with France.

In his absence France had made a few conciliatory moves, such as allowing four Tunisians to serve as ministers and giving them half the seats on the Grand Council. Neo-Destour leader Salah ben Youssef viewed these slender concessions as sops. In 1947 the new resident general, Jean Mons, granted the Tunisians six ministries. His changes were so small as to provoke scorn from the Neo-Destour, whose clandestine activities and congresses increasingly groped for independence. To the colons, however, any relaxation of control amounted to French treason.

The great evolution in the immediate postwar years lay in Neo-Destour, which redoubled its efforts on every front. By far the most important development was the construction of the national trade union, the UGTT (*Union Générale des Travailleurs Tunisiens*), in 1946. The guiding spirit in the emancipation of the Tunisian worker from the Communist-controlled French *Confédération Générale du Travail* (the CGT) and in the consolidation of the Tunisian labor movement into one powerful nationalist front was Ferhat Hached. Later to be murdered (probably by the European Red Hand terrorist society which sought to keep the Maghrib French), Hached brought the Tunisian workers into the independence movement—by 1949 the UGTT boasted almost 100,000 members. Non-industrial workers, such as farmers, artisans, and clerks, formed similar organizations.

Neo-Destour worked at every level of Tunisian society. It ministered to the poor through its solidarity committee; it published newspapers in French and Arabic; and finally, it approached the new Bey, Lamine Bey, for support of this people's party working for independence under a constitutional monarchy. By 1949 Neo-Destour claimed a half-million Tunisians for its ranks.

All this could not have been done without some official permissiveness, and Resident General Mons was subject to severe criticism by the leading colons. It is likely, however, that repression would simply have led to a more violent Tunisian counteraction and France would have faced a full-scale rebellion, out of which little cooperation or good will could have resulted.

In 1950, there began a two-year dialogue between Tunisian nationalists and France. Had a few French officials and a Tunisian delegation been able to sit down at a conference table and make binding decisions, Tunisia might have evolved toward scheduled independence. However, decisions made in France by high officials were not enforced in Tunisia, where the French civil servants formed a bloc with the colons to prevent change. On the Tunisian side, Neo-Destour was challenged here and there by Old Destour, but basically its pro gram received national support.

Early negotiations struck a promising note. Bourguiba went to Paris in April 1950, carrying a program which called for restoring a Tunisian executive, instead of having ultimate authority vested in the French office of resident general. He also asked for a Tunisian prime minister, the suppression of French control of the state administration, and removal of local government from the hands of French "civil controllers." Elected municipal authorities, in which French interests would be recognized, would manage government at a local level. He expected the French police force to yield power to a constituted Tunisian equivalent. Finally, a National Assembly, named under universal suffrage representing Tunisians and Europeans in the ratio of their true members, would draft a constitution to accommodate Tunisian sovereignty with France's special interests. All this would not appear overnight, but it was intended as an armature upon which Tunisian independence would gradually be built. Could France refuse peace-loving, French-oriented Tunisians who stood loyally by the protector in two world wars, what Libya, the less-developed eastern neighbor was promised (and given in 1951) by the United Nations?

Paris liked Bourguiba's evolutionary approach though his program was hard to take at one sitting. The colon *Rassemblement Français* did its best to block a favorable response to the Tunisian demands, but lost the first battle. The French Socialist Party, however, endorsed the idea of scheduled independence. A new resident general, Louis

Perillier, was sent to Tunis. A wise and moderate man, he sought Franco-Tunisian cooperation. Bourguiba and his Neo-Destour friends expected great things when Perillier announced (June 1950) that Tunisians would receive more administrative positions, that local government would be democratic, and that "the personality of the government" would be recreated. This announcement attracted the fire, however, of the European community in Tunisia. The French in the Grand Council resigned, and French administrators, fearing their monopoly would end if the Resident General had his way, lodged a strong protest. Paris proposed but the French in Tunisia disposed.

Even so, a new cabinet, half of whom (including the president, Mohammed Chenik) were Tunisians, took office. Salah ben Youssef, secretary general of the Neo-Destour, held the ministry of justice. Some members of the Neo-Destour and the critical Old Destour hierarchy viewed this coalition cabinet as dangerous collaboration with the French enemy. With this view Bourguiba disagreed, banking on Franco-Tunisian good will. Yet he himself refused to accept any public office, awaiting full independence before taking such a step.

What really prevented the evolution of Tunisia toward independence was powerful colon influence, both in Tunisia and in the French Assembly. In Tunisia this power expressed itself in thousands of uncooperative ways, ranging from a French administrative sabotage of Perillier's program to downright intimidation of Tunisian workers by their employers. In Paris the colon lobby, spearheaded by Senator Antoine Colonna, roared its opposition. General Alphonse Juin, born in Bône, Algeria, the son of a policeman, foresaw a diabolical plot to detach French Northwest Africa from the West and to bypass the recently built North Atlantic Treaty Organization's southern flank. He and his cohorts predicted that if French power retreated, communism would enter the vacuum.

By October, Paris ordered a slow-down on Tunisian political evolution. The reaction in Tunisia was incidents in which the French police fired upon brick-throwing Tunisian strikers. France next came up with another reform decree whose main purpose was to retain the French presence. It reduced the power of the secretary general and the chief of administration (always a Frenchman) but, because these important powers were transferred to the resident general, the change was illusory: Tunisians could work in the administration but not in the high posts. And the French kept control of local government and the police. At the highest administrative level, generous use of French veto power delayed and denied legislation which the Tunisian ministers considered vital. Private French leaders stirred up opposition groups within the Tunisian population in an effort to split the unity of Neo-Destour. Martial law, suppression of the press, and other infringements of the working contract between the French and Tunisian population, angered men of good will. Finally, in April 1951, the Bey, Premier Chenik, and Ben Youssef, the Neo-Destourian minister of justice, insisted upon full-fledged representative government.

This move took Chenik and Ben Youssef to Paris where in October they asked Foreign Minister Robert Schuman for an "exclusively Tunisian executive" and an assembly elected by universal suffrage. Two months later the French counter-proposal insisted upon continuing French participation in the "working out of the Tunisian political institutions" and the permanence of Franco-Tunisian ties.

This ended, for a time, the dialogue. Bourguiba and other Neo-Destour leaders turned away from France to the world where they prepared to state their case in the most vigorous form. France was told early in 1952 that an appeal would be made in the United Nations and, a few days later, the Security Council was asked to place the Tunisian question on the agenda.

Before anything happened at Lake Success, another wave of arrests sought to destroy the Neo-Destour's leadership. The new Resident General, Jean de Hautecloque, took seriously his orders to crush Tunisian nationalism. On January 18, 1952, Bourguiba again entered forced residence, first at Tabarka, from which he was transferred to the isolated island of Galite. Other leaders of the Neo-Destour were interned in the south. Tunisians in the Chenik ministry also felt the strong arm of the police. Ben Youssef and one of his colleagues managed to escape to Cairo where they struck up friendship and brooded over Bourguiba's position of leadership. The Bey was forced to appoint a rubber-stamp ministry under Salah Baccouche. Thus widespread terror, counter-terror, and various other forms of violence replaced the dialogue.

SIX

MOROCCAN NATIONAL CONSCIOUSNESS

1924-1952

Lyautey and His Successors

Morocco lagged behind Tunisia in becoming conscious of itself as a nation. "Young Tunisians" sowed nationalist seeds before the Treaty of Fez placed Morocco under the protectorate in 1912. During World War I, while Tunisians were thinking of programs in which they could express some political identity outside the protector's reach, Lyautey added pacified areas to French control. Morocco's self-consciousness became evident about two decades later and, due to Arab-Berber rivalry, was infinitely more complex. That there were three Moroccos—French, Spanish, and international Tangier—also complicated national unification. Finally, in a sheltered and withdrawn feudal state, traditionalism (especially religious) held back the idea of a national state in the western Maghrib.

After World War I, Marshal Lyautey found his task increasingly difficult because of the basic conflict between his conception of France's mission in Morocco, and the views of colons, administrators, and old-style politicians in France. He treated the Moroccans as his own precious children who needed time and patient care to reach maturity. He loved the people, respected their culture, and never tried to assimilate or exploit them. He stood like a powerful rock against the land-hungry colons and the entrepreneurs who came seeking fortunes for themselves, and who cared not at all for the indigenous

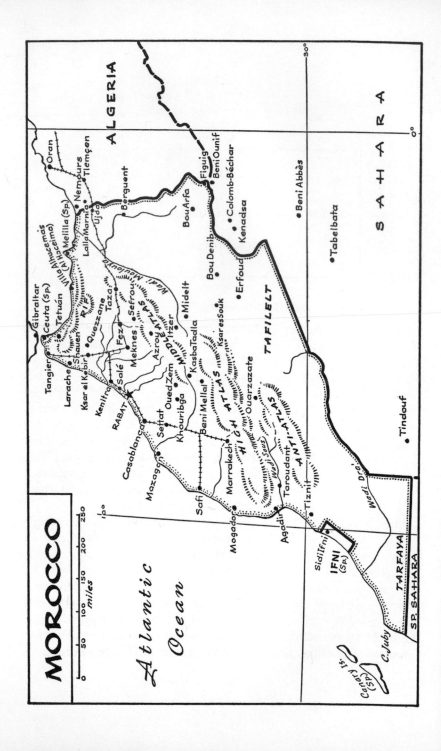

population. Respectful of the Treaty of Fez, he ruled *with* the Sultan and the Makhzan, never in place of or against it.

This happy situation could not last forever, and even if it had, there is absolutely no guarantee that Moroccan nationalism would not have been born. Had Lyautey been in command later, French reaction would no doubt have been different, and the future relationship less strained.

In 1924 Lyautey reached his seventieth year—the rock began to weather. At this time Abdelkrim, the intrepid leader of the Rif rebellion in Spanish Morocco, threatend to expand his operation into the French zone. Here was a new opponent added to those of the North African lobby in Paris, which had long demanded Lyautey's political head. After Paul Painlevé replaced Edouard Herriot as Premier of France, Marshal Pétain, "the hero of Verdun," was sent to Morocco in July 1925, to aid Lyautey in planning the campaign against Abdelkrim. On August 18, Painlevé sent Lyautey the following order: "Marshal Pétain will take over general command of the troops and military services in Morocco." A few weeks later, a major offensive of the armies of France and Spain struck against the Rifo. The plan, organization, and diplomatic preparation belonged to Lyautey, and ultimately victory fell to the French and Spanish. But on September 24, 1925, Lyautey resigned his Moroccan post.

His replacement, Theodore Steeg, schooled in administrative technique in Algeria, invoked "colonial" concepts, and in doing so discarded the great Marshal's strict adherence to the protectorate code. Lyautey's dream ended and his team of subordinates were dispersed. The new resident general studied the Moroccans on paper. He spent his time reading files and reports and seldom made human contact. He and his staff worked out policy, framed the laws, and then presented them to the Sultan for signature and seal. Administration became direct under the fiction of the protectorate.[1]

Into this changed French administrative environment came the first glimmerings of Moroccan national consciousness. Possibly it originated in a Muslim religious purification movement, the Salafi, which came out of India. These doctrines touched young Moroccans

[1] Rom Landau, *Moroccan Drama 1900-1955* (London: Robert Hale, 1956), p. 133.

such as Mohammed Lyazidi, who feared French modernism. Surely Moroccan nationalism received stimulation from conferences held in Switzerland after 1921 by Chekib Arslan, a Syrian, who preached the independence of the Maghrib to Moroccans like Mohammed al-Ouazzani and Ahmed Balafrej, who came under his influence after study in Paris.

In Fez, where the Karouane Mosque harbored a center of Islamic studies, the young scholar Allal al-Fassi and his supporters founded a club in 1926 to purify Islam. "Let us liberate our souls in order to liberate our bodies." A somewhat similar organization took shape at Rabat under the influence of Balafrej, a brilliant student at Fuad University in Cairo and the Faculty of Letters and Law at Paris, where he obtained the *diplôme d'Études Supérieurs*. By 1927 these two groups merged into the Moroccan League, dedicated to reform and progress. The Rabat group emphasized progressive democracy, while the Fez center always affirmed purified Islam. Young Moroccans opened branches of the League in many towns and even reached the countryside.

Until 1930 these intellectuals and Moroccan businessmen, who composed the driving force of the Moroccan League, had no sharply delineated goal. But in that year Resident General Lucien Saint provided the perfect target in the Berber *Dahir* (decree). On the surface no more than a judicial-administrative reform, deep down it was an unwarranted interference with Islamic religion and law. There is no doubt, too, that the French devised it to divide Arab and Berber in order to rule.

The Berber *Dahir* of 1930, signed by the seventeen-year-old Sultan Mohammed V, took the Berbers outside the jurisdiction of Islamic law, placed criminal offenses in Berber country under French courts, and recognized as judicially competent the *djemmas*. These were Berber tribal councils, previously ranked not as legal tribunes but as arbitration courts functioning in cooperation with the *Sharia*. This Islamic law, based on the Koran and various traditions, was God's law. For the infidel to interfere with it was "more . . . than a legal abuse, it was a political error." [2] General Georges Catroux later observed

[2] Charles-André Julien, *L'Afrique du Nord en marche* (Paris: Julliard, 1952), p. 146.

that Lyautey would have avoided this adventure. "He would have foreseen the moral harm that France would suffer from this action." [3] Arab and Berber alike viewed the Berber *Dahir* as a crude French interjection into the world of Islam, a world they could never understand. Although many Berbers realized that through French orders they fell under the authority of the Makhzan, a minority favored the *Dahir*.

This was France's most telling contribution to Moroccan nationalism. The Moroccan League easily demonstrated that France stood against Islam. The target had been found and soon, in the mosques, large numbers of the faithful invoked Allah not to separate them from their Berber brothers. The people joined the students, and protests too numerous to be counted took place throughout the land. All the Arab countries joined in the chant and in far away places, like the League of Nations, that chant was heard. At the United Nations in 1952 and 1953, Middle Eastern delegates told Rom Landau that the Berber *Dahir* had awakened their awareness of the Moroccan problem.[4]

Early Nationalist Activities

After 1930, nationalist awakening took many forms. The young Moroccans, led by Al-Ouazzani, Balafrej, Lyazidi, and Naciri published a newspaper (*Maghreb*) which ran two years before being suppressed in May 1934. French parties of the left, particularly the Socialist (SFIO), mildly joined the protest. In Fez, *L'Action du Peuple*, a weekly, took form under the leadership of Al-Ouazzani. It used the French Berber policy as a constant whipping post. The Paris Association of North African Students, founded in 1927, joined the cause of reform and even the Moroccan Boy Scouts marched in demonstration.

To awaken and enlist Mohammed V in the cause, the anniversaries of his accession to the throne on November 18, 1927, called forth elaborate celebrations in all the larger cities, even in Marrakech, where Al-Glawi, the Berber chief heavily favored by the French, made his capital. The "Fete of the Throne" became a national holiday. When Mohammed V visited Fez in 1934, he spoke with leaders like Al-Fassi

[3] Georges Catroux, *Lyautey le Marocain* (Paris: Hachette, 1952), p. 293.
[4] Landau, p. 147.

who explained their cause. He was a bright, well-educated, sensitive boy who had learned from his father to respect Lyautey as a fine man, devoted to Morocco's best interests. Mohammed V matured quickly and soon observed the change in French policy from protector to colonizer. He began to follow the nationalist movement closely. By keeping the palace door open to nationalist leaders, the Sultan assumed an important place in Moroccan political life. The movement needed such a symbol to be effective with the masses and on his side Mohammed V, by keeping the hearts of his people, secured his throne.

When *L'Action du Peuple* was suppressed by the French authorities in May 1934, its sponsors formed the *Comité d'Action Marocaine* (CAM). In Cairo, in September, ten CAM leaders drafted a lengthy reform proposal in Arabic. Two months later, a French version circulated in Morocco, where Mohammed V and Governor General Ponsot studied it. Obviously the proposal did not represent the thinking of the entire Moroccan people—neither did the French decrees promulgated by the Sultan's *Dahirs*—but it was a serious statement of ten leaders, among whom were Al-Fassi, Naciri, Douiri, and Al-Ouazzani.

It sought modification of the protectorate, with France's help, in the interests of the Moroccan people. The reform asked for the elimination of the authority of the grand caids, whom the French supported as part of their Berber policy of divide and rule. Local councils elected by Muslims and Jews, and by a national council, elected in two stages, the first by universal suffrage and the second by literate males, were suggested as important evolutionary steps toward more responsible government. Basic rights—freedom of expression, protection against arbitrary arrest, judicial reform, sanctity of the home, and abolition of the slave trade, which still lingered in the south—found expression in the reform.

This program, and the one of 1936, proposed unification of educational facilities. This meant the end of the separate Berber schools, part of the Berber policy of divide and rule. It asked, too, that Moroccans be given places in the administration. Greater protection of Moroccan farmers against colon penetration, and a standard agricultural credit policy which would protect the peasant against usury practiced by Muslim, Jew, and European alike, were likewise advocated.

Looking back upon the Moroccan nationalist movement from the perspective of twenty years, the crucial time lay between 1936 and 1943. These were years in which personal rivalry between leaders prevented a united front, yet these centrifugal forces were more than balanced by the opportunities opened up by World War II. No one grew more or reached out to win the support of the people more successfully, during that period, than Sultan Mohammed V.

Within the ranks of the CAM, Al-Fassi pressed his leadership against the influence of Al-Ouazzani. This rivalry, which became public in 1936, dwindled in importance when both men, along with Lyazidi, were arrested for organizing a protest rally. But General Auguste Noguès, an old Lyautey officer who became resident general a month later, freed the prisoners. Noguès also allowed meetings to be held and newspapers to be published.

Al-Fassi's group immediately founded two newspapers, El Atlas, in Arabic, directed by Lyazidi from Rabat, and L'Action Populaire, directed by Douiri, also published in Rabat. Left out of these operations, Al-Ouazzani revitalized the old L'Action du Peuple. At the base of the split stood personal rivalry, but questions of organization and tactics also divided the two leaders. Al-Fassi wanted a disciplined force under his command. Al-Ouazzani favored a loose federation of nationalist locals. Ironically, Al-Fassi, who himself emphasized the Islamic cultural base, won the support of men like Balafrej, a person who saw Paris (and the West), not Mecca, Damascus, or Cairo, as the school of ideas for the new Morocco. Balafrej understood the value of a dynamic, well-organized party of the people; therefore he supported Al-Fassi's lead. The old time café intellectuals who liked talk more than action, and individualism rather than discipline, stayed with Al-Ouazzani. Meanwhile nationalist leaders in Spanish Morocco, Abdelhaleq Torres and Naciri, used the Spanish Civil War to further their cause. When the Loyalists refused to grant independence to the Rif in exchange for support against General Franco, these men went to Franco with a similar proposition. He offered reforms, but not independence, in exchange for Moroccan soldiers.

The exact nature of the bargain between Franco and the Moroccan nationalists still remains heavily veiled. By January 1938, the Political Division of the German Foreign Office believed that 50,000 to 60,000 Moroccans served in Franco's front-line forces. Franco's ally, Nazi Germany, also showed a keen awareness of possible exploitable relationships between the Spanish Civil War and the Pan-Arab movement. Certainly Germany received important quantities of iron ore from Spanish Morocco as part payment for her military assistance. This Nazi penetration worried the Quai d'Orsay which feared another "Moroccan Crisis." [5]

In Spanish Morocco, the protector's turmoil enabled the nationalists to operate with a freer hand. Torres quickly founded the Party of National Reforms at Tetuán. This was a blow to Naciri, who wanted to be captain. So, with the help of funds advanced by the Spanish to divide the Moroccan nationalists in the Spanish zone, Naciri organized the Party of Moroccan Unity.

Unfortunately, unity within Moroccan nationalism proved elusive in the years before World War II, and, for that matter, in the years following independence. When the CAM was forced to dissolve in 1937, Al-Fassi formed the Moroccan Movement for the Plan of Reforms, while Al-Ouazzani built the Popular Movement. No serious differences crystallized by the time both the leaders went to jail in September. The French shifted over from persuasion to repression after the people of Meknes demonstrated against four colons who diverted the city's water supply. The police fired into the crowd and when the nationalists denounced this incident, their leaders were arrested. Al-Fassi was sent to Gabon, where he spent nine years of detention. Al-Ouazzani entered forced residence in the desert south.

When France marched against Nazi Germany in 1939, Mohammed V supported the Allied cause, first delegating 20,000 Moroccan soldiers to serve. After June 1940, when France fell, the Vichy regime enjoyed the full loyalty of Resident General Noguès, which meant that he tried to promulgate that regime's anti-Jewish laws in the protectorate. Mohammed V refused to sign these decrees. "Moroccan Jews are my subjects, and my duty is to protect them against any

[5] See Robert A. Friedlander, "Holy Crusade or Unholy Alliance? Franco's National Revolution and the Moors," *The Southwestern Quarterly*, XLIV (March 1964), *passim*, for excellent materials extracted from the archives and various inaccessible sources.

aggression." In November 1942, at the time of the Anglo-American landings in Morocco, Noguès ordered Franco-Moroccan resistance. This lasted three days and increased the Allies' burden. The Sultan, however, ordered his subjects to cooperate with the Americans.

De Gaulle, from London in 1941, tried to get Al-Fassi (still under close surveillance in Gabon) to use his influence in Morocco against Noguès and the Vichy regime. In return, Al-Fassi asked the Free French leader to understand the aspirations of the Moroccan people. Perhaps de Gaulle balked at this, or at the Anglo-American pressure that was put upon him to do something dramatic for the Moroccan people, but nothing came of the approach.

President Franklin Roosevelt dined with Mohammed V in Anfa, a suburb of Casablanca, on January 22, 1943. This caused great unhappiness to General Noguès and discomfort to Winston Churchill, who did not relish a non-alcoholic dinner with anyone. "Dinner, At the White House (Dry, alas!) with the Sultan." During the dinner, the President spoke favorably of a future independent Morocco, to the great satisfaction of the Sultan, who showed a remarkable interest in the United States. Later Roosevelt wrote two encouraging letters to Mohammed V and took the same general line when he visited Ibn Saud in Saudi Arabia.

Istiqlal

These events—France's collapse, the Anglo-Amercian landings, the Sultan's meeting with President Roosevelt—cheered the Moroccan nationalists, who began to bury their personal rivalries. The two factions in the Spanish zone joined in a National Pact (December 1942), and Balafrej succeeded in creating the Istiqlal, the Independence Party, in December 1943.

As its name indicates, the party's objective was no less than independence. Balafrej served as secretary general and the highest place fell to Al-Fassi, still in Gabon. Early in 1944, a manifesto asking for independence and territorial unification found its way to the desk of Resident General Gabriel Pauax, who replaced Noguès, and to the Sultan's palace.

De Gaulle's French Committee of National Liberation, based in Algiers, uttered a brisk "no" to the Manifesto. "Morocco," according to her status defined by the Treaty of Fez, "was indissolubly united to France." Pauax arrested the Istiqlal leaders on the charge of collaboration with the Germans. Balafrej ended up in Corsica, while Lyazidi and others were held locally. These acts led to massive demonstrations of disapproval in Rabat and Fez, where at least thirty Moroccans were killed, and several thousand were placed in prison. This should have ended the French "get tough" policy because, by 1944, it was perfectly clear that the protectorate could not be maintained by killing and imprisoning Moroccan nationalists. Charles-André Julien, the keen French authority on the Maghrib, considered the authoritarian protectorate "to have extended Moroccan nationalism and to have given it unity and inspiration." This repressive policy also drove the Sultan toward the cause of Istiqlal and, at the same time, it pulled the Berbers toward independence.

Istiqlal leaders asserted Morocco's cause by cable to the new United Nations at San Francisco in March 1945. At home, party organization was strengthened: the executive committee was enlarged from twelve to twenty-five, study groups took form, and new branches were founded throughout the country. Istiqlal locals sprang up even in the Berber mountain communities.

Outside Morocco, the formation of the Arab League in 1945, linking thirty-six million Arab-speaking people in the Near East, soon served as a platform from which Moroccan (and Tunisian and Algerian) nationalism could launch its case to a world audience.

Early in 1946 another resident general, Eric Labonne, came to Morocco with some new ideas. He threw out his predecessor's policy of repression, freed the political prisoners (including Al-Fassi), and embarked upon a program whose intent was to improve the lot of all Moroccans. "What matters," he told his Council, "is to give the Moroccan people, all classes thereof, the young men and women, the feeling, indeed the certainty, that no sphere of endeavor is closed to them, and that they will be given every opportunity to turn to good account their intellectual and other faculties." [6]

Labonne's reform program never had a chance because it ran into the solid opposition of the colons, the North African lobby in Paris, and the French members of the First (agricultural) and Second

[6] Quoted by Landau, p. 252.

(commerce and industry) Chambers in Morocco. Istiqlal, too, sharply criticized the educational and economic plans set forth. Even had the resident general's brave plans taken concrete shape, the Franco-Moroccan *entente* had deteriorated so far that only a complete change in attitude could restore faith. "Very few Moroccans retained by now (1946-1947), any firm belief in the good faith of France. The ulterior motive, the deceptive twist, the ambiguous phrase were all the majority expected to encounter. Nothing but fundamental change could convince them that the French had wholly honorable intentions." [7]

The Growing Influence of Mohammed V

In April 1947, Sultan Mohammed V visited Tangier, the first Sultan to do so since 1899. A few days earlier in Casablanca an incident, which started when a Senegalese soldier menaced an Arab woman, led to the death of eighty-three persons and the wounding of several hundred. This incident possibly hardened the Sultan into deleting from his Tangier speech a passage inserted by the residency, which praised the protectorate. Since the earlier version had been given to the press, the Sultan's action was blatant. He spoke, too, of "the legitimate rights of the Moroccan people." And later to the press he expressed the attachment of Morocco to the Arab League and its world of the eastern Mediterranean.

Resident General Labonne was relieved a month later and replaced by General (later Marshal) Alphonse Juin. With his colon birth and wealthy colon wife, Juin represented only too faithfully the viewpoint of his milieu. He had made an excellent record in World War I, and in World War II was given command of a motorized division. In 1941 he was released and appointed to serve Marshal Pétain. During "Operation Torch," Juin held the post of Commander-in-Chief of French Forces in North Africa, and he ordered resistance to the Anglo-American landings. Twenty-four hours later he went over to the Allies, whom he served with distinction in Tunisia, Italy, France, and Germany.

Juin reached Morocco in May 1947. By 1951, a full-fledged political crisis was brewing between France and the Sultan, who became ever more popular with the vast majority of the people. The resident gen-

[7] Landau, p. 251.

eral stated his purpose upon his arrival. "My first duty is to re-establish order, without brutality, without compulsion but with energy. . . . I shall permit no one to indulge in [demogoguery]." [8] He expected Morocco to turn toward France and could not conceive of a "viable" independent Morocco. Like most colons, he believed in "the congenital incapacity" of the Arabs.

General Juin's views are important because, supported as he was by the North African lobby in Paris and the administrative hierarchy in both Paris and Morocco, to say nothing of the colons, his decisions, unlike Labonne's, were capable of being enforced.

Despite his talent as a general, in a situation where he decided well-guided force should be used, and despite his powerful friends in Morocco, Algeria, and Paris, Resident General Juin, after four years, achieved no striking result. In truth, he failed, and the "crisis of 1951" was at hand.

The two obstacles he never surmounted, in addition to the Moroccan people whose nationalist aspiration had been kindled, were his own colon mentality and the Sultan. The lobby refused passage to Labonne's economic reform program, which Juin reasserted; and the Sultan simply refused to sign a large number of decrees in which Juin infringed upon the Sultan's authority. For example, the resident general penetrated the Makhzan, in the stated interest of better liaison, and the Sultan resented losing control over his own government. Later, the Sultan refused to sanction a change in local government procedure which granted the French inhabitants as many representatives as the Muslims, who outnumbered the French thirty-to-one. Juin, good soldier that he was, imposed a heavy censorship upon the nationalist press.

Outside French Morocco Juin had no power. He could not prevent Al-Fassi from escaping the Tangier police and reaching Cairo, where the Istiqlal leader plunged into work for the Moroccan cause. Nor could he restrain the old war horse, Abdelkrim, from jumping ship at Port Said and asking Egypt for sanctuary, so that he might escape French captivity and educate his children in the Arabic language. Cairo might seem remote from Rabat or Fez, but it was a place where

---

[8] Quoted from *Notes documentaires et études*, No. 688, Série textes et documents, CXLIX, Services Français d'Information, by Landau, p. 260.

nationalists of the Maghrib spoke to the world and laid plans for the future independence struggle. The Maghrib Office in Cairo helped convince the Arab League that the Moroccan and Tunisian questions should be heard in the United Nations. Algerian nationalists, too, of all denominations, used Cairo as a haven.

What called the attention of Paris to General Juin's failure in Morocco was a boycott staged by prominent Arab businessmen delegates of the Council in the summer of 1950. President Vincent Auriol, sensing the rising tension, invited Mohammed V to France for a state visit. The Sultan finally accepted, but warned his host that he wished political discussions. Accordingly the Sultan, between receptions, dinners, and parades, presented Auriol with a memorandum explaining the difficulties between Morocco and the French protector. The French cabinet heard these complaints and agreed to reduce censorship, legalize trade unions, and improve legal procedure.

These crumbs the Sultan accepted, but he reminded his French hosts, in a second note, that a basic change between France and the Kingdom was in order, that steps toward the abolition of the protectorate were necessary. Mohammed V never received a reply to this note. Later it was announced that a committee would study the problem. The committee never met. No *détente* was reached in Paris. General Juin continued on his way, and the Sultan returned to Casablanca to a welcoming multitude, including bands of Berbers who rode all the way from the Atlas to show their respect for the way in which he stood up to the protector. Mohammed V never lacked courage.

The so-called "Crisis of 1951," which was entirely political in nature, began in December 1950 at the session of the Government Council, where elected Moroccan representatives hammered French policy. Ahmed Lyazidi, President of the Federation of Moroccan Chambers of Commerce, was silenced for observing that the protectorate's financial policy only benefited French interests. Later, General Juin ordered Mohammed Laghzaoui out of both the room and the Council. Nine important delegates, all members of Istiqlal, followed him. Later the same day they called upon the Sultan.

Resident General Juin immediately turned to Thami al-Glawi, the Pasha of Marrakech, for Berber support against the Sultan. Within a few days Al-Glawi accused Mohammed V of being, not the Sultan of Morocco, but the "Sultan of the Istiqlal." The Sultan ordered him out of the palace. Al-Glawi, at Juin's suggestion, toured the Berber villages where he asked the caids to support him against the Sultan. Petitions against Istiqlal and the Sultan were circulated by tribal leaders and French officials. Berber horsemen later marched to Fez and Rabat under various pretexts. Their leaders and French officials told them they would receive anti-tuberculosis vaccinations, gifts of sugar, and feasts. Later General Juin called the Berber presence in the cities "a spontaneous uprising of the Moroccan people."

In January 1951, General Juin strongly insisted that Mohammed V sign the major *Dahirs* which lay on the table and that he publicly denounce Istiqlal. The Sultan asked Juin to let the courts handle any misdeeds of Istiqlal. The Resident General replied with this ultimatum: "You either condemn the Istiqlal or you renounce your throne. Otherwise I shall depose you myself. I am now leaving for Washington. You have time enough to think over my request. We shall see, on my return, what is to be done." [9]

Off went General Juin to Washington where American officials who were responsible for building air bases in Morocco advised him to be more reasonable. In Paris Juin's actions received the support of the majority of the cabinet, including Premier Pleven and Interior Minister Queuille; Robert Schuman, foreign minister, and Jules Moch, minister of national defense, opposed Juin's policy.

By February, Resident General Juin had increased his demands upon the Sultan. Members of Istiqlal were to be expelled from the Islamic community of the faithful as atheists. Mohammed V convened the Makhzan, and the religious leaders, *ulema*, who unanimously agreed that there was no legal basis in Islamic law or the Treaty of Fez for outlawing the Istiqlal. Nor could the Sultan "excommunicate" the Istiqlal membership and remain the religious leader.

By this time the Berber horsemen, who had come into Fez and Rabat for sugar and vaccinations, were camped at the city gates. General Juin again ordered the Sultan to accept his demands or abdicate. Mohammed V signed, as he said, under duress and to avoid bloodshed. His earlier telegram to President Vincent Auriol brought

[9] Quoted by Landau, p. 275, from the verbatim report received from the palace.

the reply that he should compromise. General Juin chalked up a victory which soon proved to be extremely costly.

Instead of protecting the Sultan, as the Treaty of Fez provided, the French Resident General threatened him with his own people, most of whom had been duped into riding to Fez and Rabat. When the tribesmen realized this, they asked that their caids, who had misled them, be replaced. The net result, then, was a rallying of the Berbers to their Sultan. As for the Istiqlal, its leaders landed in jail once again. Included in the round-up were Mohammed Lyazidi, Amar Abdeljalil, Abdelkrim Bendjelloun and Mehdi Ben Barka. Various minor nationalist parties reacted positively, stopped bickering, and in April 1951, at Tangier, they formed a united front behind Istiqlal's banner. These nationalists stood for independence, no union with France, cooperation with the Arab League, and no cooperation with the communists. This Pact of Tangier, signed by Al-Fassi, Al-Ouazzani, Torres, and Naciri, formed the Moroccan National Front.

SEVEN

THE UNITED NATIONS AND MILITANT
NATIONALISM IN MOROCCO AND
TUNISIA 1952-1954

Tunisian and Moroccan nationalists, by 1952, held in common the ultimate objectives of independence, but they differed considerably in their approach. Neo-Destour, which occasionally resorted to massive protest (sometimes ending in violence), usually followed the path of nonviolence. Istiqlal was more forthright in demanding independence and its leaders were men steeped in Islamic faith and Arabic culture. The Moroccan movement possessed a fiery quality, which the Tunisian movement lacked. Perhaps Morocco's location, in the front line of the ancient struggle between the cross and the crescent, contributed to this characteristic. Its large Berber population and the French Berber policy added fuel to the fire.

Tunisian leaders like Bourguiba knew the West better than the Near East, where the Moroccan leaders naturally gravitated for support. And the Tunisians pushed their cause on to the world stage earlier, largely because of the travel and education of Bourguiba.

Appeals to the United Nations

By the autumn of 1952, however, both nationalist movements gained a hearing in the United Nations. Earlier the Neo-Destour established information offices in Jakarta, New Delhi, Baghdad, and New York. And the Tunisian trade union, UGTT, had joined the International Confederation of the Free Trade Unions, where its leader, Ferhat Hached, found a receptive audience. At Milan, in

1951, he spoke impressively. American trade union leaders invited him to address the AF of L Convention in San Francisco the following year. The Moroccan Office opened in Washington in 1951, under the supervision of Dr. Mehdi ben Aboud. Late that same year Egypt asked the UN General Assembly, then meeting in Paris, to discuss the "Violation of the Principles of the Charter and of the Declaration of Human Rights by France in Morocco." The General Committee voted to postpone the discussion.

Tunisia had earlier, as we have seen, politely informed France that it would appeal its case to the Security Council meeting in Paris. This was done by Ben Youssef and Mohammed Badra on January 14, 1952. New Resident General Hautecloque asked the Bey to withdraw the appeal. When the Bey refused, Hautecloque came down with a heavy hand. He banned the Neo-Destour congress, arrested and exiled its leaders, and banned the UGTT anniversary celebration. The climax came in "operation mop-up" at the end of January 1952, when French troops, ordered to reduce nationalist activity, took an untold number of lives and destroyed many Tunisian homes. This provoked Tunisian counter-terror which continued for some sixty days. Hautecloque finally forced the Bey to dissolve the Chenik ministry in favor of the puppet Baccouche.

On April 2, 1952, eleven Afro-Asian states demanded that the Tunisian question be placed on the Security Council's agenda. The motion was killed. In the discussion, the United States favored continuation of talks between France and Tunisia. Unsatisfied, the Afro-Asian states tried to schedule a special summer meeting of the General Assembly. When this maneuver failed, the Tunisian and Moroccan petitions were definitely placed on the agenda for the fall session of 1952, to be held in New York.

Relationships between the French protector and the Moroccan and Tunisian nationalists deteriorated during the spring and summer of 1952. In Morocco, General Guillaume, who replaced General Juin as resident general, continued his predecessor's policy. The Sultan petitioned President Auriol for removal of the state of siege and for discussions which would clearly define the protectorate's powers. The Sultan referred to his memorandum of 1950 as a basis for talks. No reply came from Paris.

In Tunisia a similar drift toward violence ensued, characterized by increased terrorism and counter-terrorism. Unexplained bombs exploded near suspected meeting places of the Neo-Destour. This atmosphere in Tunisia and Morocco more than counterbalanced any reform measures suggested by France. In both protectorates the colons fought against what they considered the tidal wave of independence which would drown them and inundate their property. It was perfectly true, by this time, that the nationalists in both protectorates sought ultimate independence.

But to calm the shattered colon nerves, *Al Istiqlal*, the weekly paper in Morocco, in its March 29, 1952 issue recognized French rights and interests and promised to guarantee them in a convention. "There is no question of a complete break with France. On the contrary, our aim is to insure the continuation of Franco-Moroccan relations, but within a framework that gives satisfactory scope to the aspirations of the Moroccan people." [1] France kept offering administrative changes and reforms which were based upon the "co-sovereignty" principle. Neither the Moroccans nor the Tunisian leaders accepted the view that the protectorate treaties entitled France to "co-sovereignty." In defense of his position, the Sultan could cite the decision of August 27, 1952, handed down by the Hague International Court of Justice. This case involved American treaty rights before 1912; the court held that Morocco still possessed sovereignty.

Both the Tunisian and Moroccan questions reached the United Nations' floor in December 1952. France always denied the competence of that world organization to concern itself with such "domestic" matters. The moment these items were posted for discussion at New York, colon reactions in both areas moved into high gear. The Tunisian issue reached the Political and Security Committee on December 4, 1952. The following day the UGTT leader, Ferhat Hached, was murdered in a Tunis suburb. Moroccan workers retaliated with a protest riot in Casablanca.

The Arab-Asian resolution, calling for negotiations between France and the "true representatives of the Tunisian people" to fulfill self-determination and the national aspirations of the Tunisians, and asking for a "good offices" committee of three to aid negotiations,

[1] Quoted by Hahn, p. 101, and Landau, p. 285.

failed by a vote of 27 to 24, with seven abstentions. The United States and the United Kingdom voted, along with the French NATO ally, against the resolution. A watered-down Latin-American resolution, calling for direct Franco-Tunisian negotiations, passed 45 to 3, with ten abstentions.

The Moroccan item came up for discussion on December 13, at the moment of widespread demonstrations in Morocco. Heavy repression took an untold number of lives and led to the arrest of hundreds, perhaps thousands, of Istiqlal members. The resolution asked for negotiations between the Sultan and France in the interest of fulfilling Moroccan aspirations and recognizing Moroccan sovereignty. It, too, lost. The Moroccan delegation, with Al-Fassi, Balafrej, and Laghzaoui of Istiqlal, Ben Souda Al-Ouazzani, and Cherkaoui of the PDI, the Democratic Independence Party, a splinter of Istiqlal, Naciri of the PMU, Party of Moroccan Unity, and Bennouna of the PRN, offered convincing proof that the Moroccan National Front spoke for an important sector of the people.

Both North African delegations and their party supporters were keenly disappointed with these results, although even a favorable vote in the UN for the strong resolutions would have had little, if any, official effect upon France. What was more important than the Tunisians and Moroccans perhaps understood, was that their cases had come to the attention of the entire world. Even in countries like the United States and the United Kingdom, whose votes in the UN were determined largely by world strategy and the preservation of NATO's unity, a warm sympathy had been kindled, if not officially in Washinton or Downing Street, then, more importantly, with the discerning reader who began to follow these questions and whose interest itself could be of value in reaching a solution. The democratic dream that people still had some influence upon events, that power groups could be limited, had some validity even in the big, mechanized, impersonal world of the mid-twentieth century.

France's official posture remained unchanged. The policy of force would be continued, but in France important people and a goodly section of the masses looked upon that policy as bankrupt. After this first hearing in the UN, the entire world would be more alert and more critical of the unfolding events.

In Tunisia, Resident General Hautecloque proceeded to hold elections, which the Neo-Destour boycotted because they were held under conditions of martial law and widespread intimidation. Despite the large resources used by the Residence to get the voters out, a scant 10 per cent of the eligible voters bothered with the empty formality. Finally, after more repression, Hautecloque was replaced by the more conciliatory Pierre Voizard. This did not prevent the assassination of Hedi Chakir, a member of the political bureau of Neo-Destour, probably by Red Hand gangsters. Voizard freed nationalist leaders, and men like Mongi Slim worked for new conversations with the protector.

The Dethronement of Mohammed V

Meanwhile, in Morocco, 1953 became a year of French disaster and led directly to rebellion. The target, as in 1951, was Sultan Mohammed V, who still refused to sign French-drawn decrees which further eroded his sovereignty. Al-Glawi, aided by French officials and encouraged by the colons, obtained signatures from some three hundred caids on a petition denouncing the Sultan and Istiqlal. Sherif Abdelhay Kittani, leader of the Kittaniya brotherhood and sworn enemy of Mohammed V (one of whose ancestors had executed Kittani's grandfather), convened the North African Brotherhoods to denounce the Sultan. With French help Al-Glawi whipped up the Berber tribesmen and Kittani organized religious opposition. The 318 ulema, the learned doctors of Islamic law, supported the Sultan.

The hard fact was that Resident General Guillaume followed General (now Marshal) Juin's program, which the Sultan blocked. The Sultan had to go, so Al-Glawi's "feudal conspiracy" furnished the cause and the troops. The *Tribune des Nations* in Paris believed "the 270 pashas and caids who requested that the French government dismiss the Sultan, by no means represent[ed] the Berber populations of Morocco; for the most part they [were] officials chosen by the French administration." [2] The exactions of these southern feudalists were a scandal. Al-Glawi held enormous power in his bailiwick around Marrakech, power which he abused, as he "ate the people under him."

[2] Quoted by Landau, pp. 302-303.

Though Al-Glawi held a veritable strangle-hold upon the economy of his fief, he was a heavy spender and usually kept himself in debt. His degrading participation in prostitution further alienated, not simply the French Catholics of the district, but also many Moroccans. Robert Barrat, the French author whose articles appeared in *Esprit* and *Témoignage Chrétien* wrote of these white-slave activities. "Every year he claims so many young women from the tribes under his authority to provide his houses with fresh white cargo. The number of prostitutes installed in his 'houses' is estimated at 4000. He receives 100 francs per day and per head from the commerce in their charms." [3] The *mission civilisatrice* had strange bedfellows and curious ways.

The dethronement of Mohammed V came swiftly. General Guillaume served the Sultan an ultimatum to sign all the pending decrees. When the Sultan refused, Al-Glawi announced that the Moroccan people no longer recognized him. By August 20, 1953, Berber tribesmen moved into Rabat and Fez and French soldiers disarmed the palace guard. The royal family was taken into custody by French officials and flown to Corsica, thence to Madagascar. Mohammed V's elderly uncle, Moulay ben Arafa, who was also Al-Glawi's son-in-law, became the puppet Sultan. Moulay ben Arafa obediently signed all the decrees drafted by the French administration, and, had not the Moroccan people resisted, the protectorate would have become a tightly bound colony.

Even though the United Nations in its eighth session (1953) refused to endorse various strongly-worded resolutions favoring the evolution of Morocco toward independence, the end of martial law, and free elections, and the dethronement of Mohammed V met nation-wide protest in Morocco. In the Spanish Zone, High Commissioner Garcia Valino declined to recognize the deposition, the *Khalifa* of Tetuán refused to change loyalties, and the Muslim flock said prayers in the name of Sidi Mohammed ben Youssef, the more intimate and endearing name of Mohammed V. Spanish Morocco opened its doors to refugees from General Guillaume's police squads

[3] Quoted from Robert Barrat, *Justice pour le Maroc* (Paris: Editions du Seuil, 1953), p. 73; by Landau, p. 299.

and no extradition was allowed. Meanwhile, General Franco sent delegations to the Arab League whose press hailed him as "a true friend of the Muslims." Torres, the nationalist leader, returned to the Spanish zone from Tangier. In short, Spain tried to profit from the French folly. Nationalists entered the government for the first time. Spain hoped, through leniency, to hold the line against the independent movement. This hope could never stand up against the nationalist drive for territorial unification; but it did mean that Spain left a smaller legacy of bitterness when the end came.

From inside French Morocco, the reaction of the masses was far more important than the maneuvering of the Caudillo and Valino in the Spanish zone. The French anticipated (and prepared for) immediate violent reaction to the dethronement. They were wrong. Sidi Mohammed simply became a "martyr and a saint." Large numbers of Moroccans "saw" the Sultan's image in the moon. At night, crowds stood looking upward into the sky communicating, in a mystical way, with the deposed Sultan.

Within a few months, the Moroccan resistance took form. Although Balafrej escaped to New York and Al-Fassi was safe in Cairo, the leaders of Istiqlal were in prison. This left command in the hands of younger men, who decided to fight violence with violence. The tactics were strictly hit-and-run, and the targets most often were not French but Moroccan informers, police agents, and persons known to be unsympathetic to the nationalist cause. Muslims refused to enter mosques where prayers could not be said for Sidi Mohammed. Imams resigned, rather than mention the puppet Sultan Moulay ben Arafa. Early in 1954 French goods came under boycott. The tobacco monopoly always produced an important revenue, so the Moroccans stopped smoking, reducing tobacco sales by nearly 80 per cent. French property in the form of harvested grain, stores, and automobiles mysteriously caught fire. Trains were derailed.

In March, Nobel Laureate François Mauriac wrote from Paris, in *France-Maghrib*, a publication he had helped to found in the interest of better understanding between the French and the people of Northwest Africa:

> Sidi Mohammed ben Youssef was never stronger than he is today. We are more dependent on him than he is on us. We only hold his body

captive; but he holds the spirit and heart of the millions of Moroccans who, a fact without precedence, go so far as to refuse to pray, since they are forbidden to pray in his name.[4]

Riding against this religio-nationalist tide were Moulay ben Arafa, who signed everything the Residence put on his desk—even at one point a menu—and Al-Glawi's faction, which was not large. In general, the Berbers rallied, if not to Istiqlal, to the deposed Sultan. Dethronement, more than any other French activity, made them consciously Moroccans.

France Changes Tactics

France faced some serious decisions early in 1954. In Indo-China, an eight-year colonial struggle reached crisis proportions; in Tunisia the hoped-for amelioration between Resident General Voizard and Neo-Destour failed to materialize, and in Morocco, turmoil became the order of the day. Could France afford a policy of force in three theaters? Wisdom dictated the abandonment of force; tactics suggested reducing the zone of the Afro-Asian battleground.

In Tunisia, the new reform program of March 1954, which might have been warmly received by the nationalists five years earlier, was quickly dismissed by moderate Neo-Destourians as inadequate. They demanded the direction of, not cooperation in, political affairs, and they also insisted upon the control of public security. Another frustration arose when members of Neo-Destour were appointed to the cabinet of Mohammed M'zali.

In the spring of 1954, the party's moderate approach wore thin. The younger members saw no future in the new dialogue with France, which took so long to yield so little. Accordingly, they selected the mountains of southern Tunisia as a stronghold from which guerrilla warfare could be launched. Publicly, Neo-Destour denied any association with this violence; actually, however, *fellaghas* (bandits to the French, guerilla fighters to the Tunisians) were recruited in party headquarters in various cities. They quickly made their presence felt, to the inconvenience of the French administration and armed forces.

The accession of Pierre Mendès-France to the premiership of France on June 20, 1954, brought a breath of fresh air to the humid

[4] March 1954 issue, quoted by Landau, p. 324.

jungle of politics in the Fourth Republic. Brilliant, astute, courageous, and impatient, he had known the leaders of the Tunisian students in Paris and had learned from young men like Mohammed Masmoudi about their attitudes and hopes. He agreed without emotionalism that France's best course lay in granting internal autonomy in Tunisia. Then, when independence came, economic and cultural relationships would continue under favorable conditions. Political control would revert to Tunisia; French influence would increase.

He sold his cabinet these ideas, and, on July 31, 1954, he went to Carthage, taking Marshal Juin along as a shield against the colons. Here he told the Bey that France stood ready to return internal sovereignty to Tunisia. Bourguiba, still in French custody, was allowed to communicate with Neo-Destour and French leaders, and his residence was made more comfortable.

The Bey appointed a new government, headed by Tahar ben Ammar, not a member of Neo-Destour, but acceptable to the party. With him, served four party members: Mongi Slim and Mohammed Masmoudi (ministers of state), Hedi Nouira (commerce), and Sadok Mokaddam (justice). Slim, Masmoudi, and Abdelaziz Djelloui (health) formed the Tunisian delegation to negotiate with France. Christian Fouchet, French Minister of Moroccan and Tunisian Affairs, paved the way by recognizing the legality of Neo-Destour.

Negotiating Tunisian autonomy after the French presence of seventy-five years was exceedingly difficult. Many complex, emotionally-loaded questions required solution: (1) rights of Tunisians and Frenchmen in Tunisia and rights of Tunisians in France; (2) cooperation in administrative and technical matters; (3) France's rights in handling foreign relations; (4) judicial questions; (5) cultural, economic, and fiscal relationships; (6) France's military rights.

The answers to these questions affected both Tunisia's and France's future dealings with Morocco. Whatever concessions Tunisia exacted, Morocco surely would demand the same. And Tunisia had to be careful to drive a hard bargain, since other Arab states were still in the process of seeking autonomy. Mendès-France tried to soften the Moroccan reaction by appointing a new Moroccan Resident General, Francis Lacoste, a diplomat, in place of General Guillaume. At the same time administrative and economic reforms were promised, but no one offered to bring back the deposed Sultan. Imprisoned nationalist leaders, like Lyazidi and Ben Barka, gained their freedom, but these men, far from being grateful, harbored deep resentment. Ben Barka had been in prison four years without being formally charged with a crime. Upon release, his first formal statement singled out Mohammed V as Morocco's only legitimate spokesman.

The most serious complication entered the French Northwest African picture on November 1, 1954, when violence broke out at seventy widely separated points in Algeria. French authorities at first underestimated the seriousness of the rebellion, destined to last for seven years and four months. The immediate effect of this uprising, which quickly became a full-scale revolution, was to speed French efforts to solve the problems of Tunisia and Morocco. Tunisia became autonomous in June 1955, and independent, along with Morocco, in March 1956.

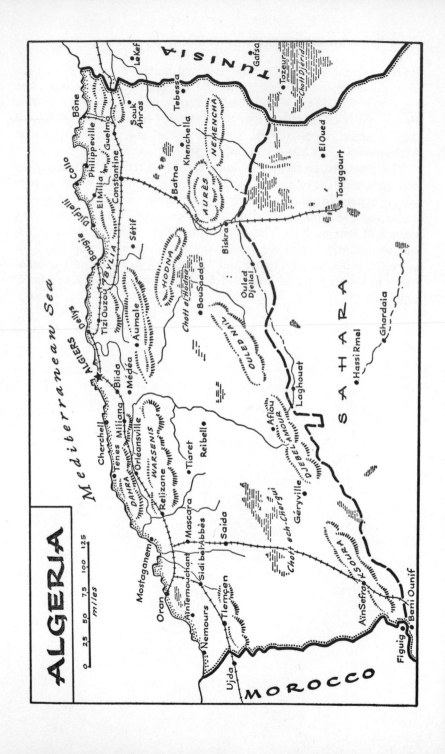

EIGHT

ALGERIAN NATIONALISM

1925-1954

Chronologically, Algerian national consciousness appeared after that of Tunisia and before that of Morocco, showing a similar awareness. Two world wars speeded the process by calling on Algerian soldiers, armored divisions, and factories. In World War II, Algerians of all classes met large numbers of Anglo-American soldiers, observed their ways, and compared them with the French counterpart and master. The elite read the Atlantic Charter and hoped its brave statement would not die as words alone, a clever bit of wartime propaganda, concocted by the beleaguered Allies.

Algerian nationalism contained a quality different from that of Tunisia and Morocco, and it evolved in a clearly European-dominated environment. Three of its four roots evolved, at least in part, out of France itself. Messali Hadj's *Étoile Nord-Africaine,* founded in 1925, recruited its members in the industrial outskirts of Paris. In 1930, another movement, whose leaders were French-oriented Muslims, like Ferhat Abbas, formed the Federation of Elected Muslims, from among local office-holders. In 1931, Abbas wrote, in *The Young Algerian,* "Algeria is French territory. We are Frenchmen with Muslim personal status." The Communists made a third group, motivated from Europe. They began an Algerian federation as early as 1924. The Algerian Communist Party took form ten years later and had small influence on the course of events.

The Muslim-Arab thrust in Algerian nationalism came from the

99

ulema, learned teachers of religion and law, who, beginning around 1930, combatted the debased doctrines of the semi-educated *mara-bouts* (self-designated holy men who acted in the French interest), by their teaching in Koranic schools. The ulema always insisted that their doctrines contained no political content, but such a separation could never be made in Islam. In 1935, the Association of Algerian Ulema, under Abd al-Hamid Ben Badis, was organized. Such slogans as "Islam is our religion, Algeria our country, Arabic our language," gave nationalist impact to their thought and action. The French tried to reduce this influence by depriving ulema of the use of state mosques, and screening the teachers whose sermons contained anti-French overtones.

Between assimilationists like Ferhat Abbas and Islamic-oriented Ben Badis, sharp differences appeared in the open by 1936. Abbas denied the existence of the Algerian nation.

If I had discovered the *Algerian nation,* I would be a nationalist and I would not blush for my crime. Men who die for the patriotic ideal are daily honored and respected. My life is not worth any more than theirs. However, I will not die for the *Algerian fatherland* because this *fatherland* does not exist. I have not found it. I questioned history, I questioned the living and the dead; I visited the cemeteries; no one spoke to me of it. . . . One cannot build on the wind. We have discarded once and for all the nonsense and chimeras to align our future definitely with that of the French work in the country. . . . No outsider believes seriously in our nationalism. What we really seek behind this word is our economic and political emancipation. Without the emancipation of the indigenous inhabitants there can be no lasting French Algeria.[1]

Two months later, Ben Badis issued the clearly nationalist ulema reply.

We have searched in history and in the present and we have undeniably established that the Algerian Muslim nation is formed and exists, as all the other nations of the world. This nation has its history demonstrated by facts; it has religious and linguistic unity; it has its culture,

[1] Quotation from Abbas by Charles-André Julien, *L'Afrique du Nord en marche, nationalismes musulmans et souveraineté française* (Paris: Julliard, 1952), pp. 110-111, from *L'Entente,* February 23, 1936.

traditions, and characteristics, good or bad, as is the case for any nation on earth. Further, we say that this Algerian nation is not France, cannot be France, and does not wish to be France. It is impossible that it be France, even if it wished assimilation. It has its fixed territory which is Algeria with its present boundaries.[2]

In Algeria, the Europeans made up a much larger fraction of the population (10 per cent in 1954) than in Tunisia or Morocco. At that time many families were four generations removed from their "pioneer" ancestors who came from France to Algeria. Their spokesmen in the twentieth century had gained an autonomy from France which they refused to share with the Muslims, and, as for assimilation or the later equivalent, "integration," these were not much more than words to insure the continued dominance of the Europeans. They talked about assimilation and integration but their practices came remarkably close to an *apartheid* program.

In 1919 the colons fought, unsuccessfully as it turned out, Clemenceau's program extending citizenship to a limited number of Algerians whose loyalty was proven by military service for France or in other concrete ways. This was a reward, like the Legion of Honor, not a right, yet the colons saw it as a dangerous opening of the flood gates. They had opposed the drafting of Muslims into the French army in 1914—it might lead to insurrection and surely would destroy the labor market!

Later, in 1937, the Popular Front's effort to conciliate Algerian moderates like Dr. Benjelloul and Ferhat Abbas, ran against the solid rock of colon opposition. On the advice of Maurice Violette, who served as governor general in Algeria (1925-1927), Premier Léon Blum endorsed the principle of extending political rights to certain distinguished Algerians without asking them to renounce their Muslim status or the jurisdiction of Koranic law. The Blum-Violette proposal sought in the first year of its application to admit 21,000 Muslims to full French citizenship. This idea, which echoed Lyautey's thinking, would have brought into the French body politic Muslim soldiers, teachers, officials, and holders of degrees from French schools. Spokesmen for the colons stated flatly: "Since 1919 we have extended maximum concessions. We should not be asked to go further because

[2] Quoted by Julien, p. 115, from *Ach Chihab*, April 1936.

it is impossible." Three hundred mayors in Algeria endorsed this view. The Blum-Violette plan died on the vine, but it surely would not have solved the Algerian problem had it become law. It might, however, have tempered the extremists among nationalists and Europeans by a gradualism which demonstrated that the two communities could live together without violence, without a ratio of 10 per cent freemen, or masters, and 90 per cent slaves.

The colon mentality deserves close study. It was based upon fear, racialism, rugged individualism, paternalism, and a considerable amount of courage and ignorance. Like a Damoclean sword, the fear that someday Muslims would find weapons and use them on the masters, hung over the Europeans. Their control was based upon force and, they believed, the superiority of their civilization. They would accept nothing which might change the balance. There could be no guns for the Muslims and very few educational opportunities. Jean Daniel, writing in the French weekly, *L'Express* on June 4, 1955, drew a comparison.

> These French of Algeria have more than one point in common with the Southerners (*esclavigistes*) of the United States: courage, dynamism, narrowness of views, the sincere conviction that they are born to be masters as others are born to be slaves . . . and affection for servants if they wish to remain servants. . . .

In speaking of their treatment of the Muslims to Americans, the colons often argued that they might have exterminated the Muslims and saved themselves a great deal of trouble, as the Americans did in the case of the American Indian. This was an attitude which demonstrated some ignorance and which showed no understanding of the passage of time. The American Indian had not been exterminated, though he was dispossessed and very badly treated. But a bad nineteenth-century solution to a twentieth-century problem was unlikely to work. And if the colons had exterminated the Muslim, who would have provided the cheap labor force? One reason the Muslim was feared by the colon was that the colon had traditionally treated him as subhuman. If the Muslim came into power, he might act in the same way, and brutally dispossess the French. If this should happen "Gros colons" (large entrepreneurial French Algerians) had less to worry about when they returned to the other side of the Mediterranean than did the little colons and "poor whites." The small farmer shared most of the big colons' attitudes, especially after the rebellion began. He would find competition very difficult if he returned landless to France. There it was more expensive to keep a servant. In fact the "poor white" might have to go into service himself in mainland society. His French status would be considerably lower than his Algerian status.

The French who controlled Algeria were never easier in their minds about the Muslims than during the Vichy period (1940-1943). The anti-Jewish legislation of Vichy came to Algeria, and the Crémieux law, which granted Jews full French citizenship, was revoked. The Jews fell back into the position occupied by the Muslims. Muslim political leaders, trade unionists, in fact troublesome Muslims of any kind, were simply tossed into jails or camps where they were found by Anglo-American journalists who arrived with "Operation Torch" late in 1942. Messali Hadj went to prison in March 1941.

The Algerian Manifesto

On February 12, 1943, a dozen Muslim leaders, including Ferhat Abbas, issued the "Manifesto of the Algerian People." It called attention to the plight of the great mass of Muslims. Abandoning the policy of assimilation as a failure, it sought federal autonomy within the French system. On the positive side, the Manifesto suggested reforms to equalize the Arabo-Berber population's rights, privileges, and duties with those of the Europeans. The foundation stone of the new order was a governing statute which guaranteed absolute liberty and equality without distinction as to race or religion. From this base, the Manifesto shaped a broad agrarian reform to re-establish Muslims on the land; it also demanded recognition of Arabic, along with French, as an official language. It stood for liberty of the press, association, and free obligatory instruction for all children. Nowhere was independence mentioned. Nor did Pan-Arabism creep in. Actually a statement endorsing freedom of religion under the principle of separation of church and state seemed both European and secular.

This brave statement and a supplement added on May 26 ultimately came to rest on the desk of General Georges Catroux, who was made Governor General of Algeria on June 3, 1943, under the authority of the French Committee of National Liberations, in which de Gaulle and General Henri Giraud served as co-chairmen.[3] Catroux turned thumbs down on the Manifesto and placed Saydah Abdel-kader and Ferhat Abbas under forced residence. Fear of colon reaction plus the demands of the war-effort no doubt entered into this decision.

De Gaulle disassociated himself completely from the Vichy administration in Algeria which had promised the Muslims very little beyond domination of the Europeans, anti-Jewish legislation, and prison for any Muslim or Jewish leaders who spoke out against their strait-jacket. On December 12, 1943, at Constantine, de Gaulle promised the Muslims certain reforms.

This promise he fulfilled in an Ordinance dated March 7, 1944. Sixteen categories of Muslims obtained full French citizenship, at the same time retaining their personal status. Muslim high school and college graduates, former army officers, decorated war veterans, administrators, members of economic commissions, in all, some 60,000, joined the first electoral college, previously exclusively reserved for Frenchmen. Muslim males over the age of twenty-one not included in the first college, some 1,500,000 persons, received the right to vote within the second college. "Lastly, the proportion of those elected to the second college in the assemblies, including the French Parliament, would be increased to parity." [4]

This Ordinance returned to the policy of progressive assimilation—to the Blum-Violette proposal of 1937. The important question was, would a 1937 answer be acceptable to a 1944 question? The Ordinance satisfied only the most Francophile Muslim leaders. The colons, of course, hated it. And, once de Gaulle went to France, they were relatively free to kill the spirit and the letter of the new policy. Both the Party of the Algerian People, which is what Messali Hadj's *Étoile Nord-Africaine* had become, and the Friends of the Manifesto and Liberty led by Ferhat Abbas objected that the Ordinance did not treat all Algerians equally and it did not extend enough responsibility

[3] Arthur Layton Funk, *Charles de Gaulle, the Crucial Years* (1943-1944) (Norman, Okla.: University of Oklahoma Press, 1959), p. 127.

[4] Charles de Gaulle, *The War Memoirs of Charles de Gaulle: Unity, 1942-1944,* translated by Richard Howard (New York: Simon and Schuster, 1959), p. 206.

to them. They posted a resolution denouncing colonialism and stated their goal "to make familiar the idea of an Algerian nation, to support an autonomous federal republic in Algeria federated to a revived, anticolonial, anti-imperialist French Republic." [5]

Tension mounted, in the spring of 1945, between advanced elements of the Algerian nationalists and the colons. The colons, who generally disliked de Gaulle and his work, turned their wrath upon the new governor general, Yves Chataigneau, who had relieved Catroux the previous September. They accused the Governor General of being too sympathetic to Islamic culture, too respectful of Muslims, and worse, too popular with them. So the colons called him "Chataigneau ben Mohammed," and awaited an opportunity to ship him back to France. Muslim extremists were equally restless. They knew that the war's end would freeze the situation and some of them dreamed of a resurrected Arab state. Chataigneau alerted his prefects against impending violence, and he was quite correct, for on May 8, 1945 (in Sétif), an incident, which marked the watershed between peaceful evolution and militant reaction, took place. Call it a "point of no return" or an experience which, as many Algerian revolutionary leaders later noted, separated the men from the boys and led the men toward direct action against the French, in whom they had lost all confidence.

A victory parade of Muslims, authorized by the underprefect, carried the Algerian red, white, and green flag—across which, such inscriptions as "Long Live Independent Algeria," "Down with Colonialism," "Down with the Communist Party," and "Free Messali Hadj" were displayed. Someone tried to grab these banners and someone else opened fire with small arms. The crowd panicked. The first count indicated thirty dead. That night buildings were attacked by Muslims and by the time peace was restored, possibly one hundred Europeans were dead.

No more than 5 per cent of the Muslims in the Constantine took part in these violent events. Still, understandably, the Europeans were apprehensive and angry. A kind of "great fear" filled the countryside, only this time the brigands were expected to be wild-eyed Arabs with sharp knives.

[5] Quoted by Julien, pp. 299-300.

French military and police forces moved quickly to quell the uprising. In Sétif, which was placed under martial law, any Muslim found without the identifying arm band was shot. The French cruiser "Duguay-Trouin" needlessly shelled the outskirts of Kerrata while the air force, flying American-built medium and light bombers given for use against the Axis, wiped out crowded Arab housing areas. *Stars and Stripes*, the American army newspaper, reported that the French air force sometimes flew three hundred sorties a day and had killed or wounded more than 10,000 Muslims in nine days. "During the campaign the Senegalese and Foreign Legion troops pillaged, burned, violated, and killed in complete liberty." [6] Estimates of the Muslim death toll vary from 1500, the official figure, to 45,000, the Algerian nationalist figure. Forty-five hundred arrests were made, 99 persons condemned to death, and 64 given life in prison. Proof of guilt rarely existed. Membership in one of the Algerian political parties was enough to lead to arrest. Ferhat Abbas and Dr. Saadane of the Association of the Friends of the Manifesto and Liberty landed in jail.

No one profited from the Sétif uprising and its pitiless repression. Chataigneau, who for nearly three years afterwards tried to forward his rural amelioration plan, profited least of all. His plan, however, provided agricultural education for Muslim farmers and succeeded in developing eighty-five modern agricultural sectors which raised cereals and fruit. New classrooms were built and rural industry received a consideration and strengthening. This excellent program was not forgotten but, unfortunately, neither was the repression. The whip and the helping hand exposed the kind of schizophrenia which characterized the French policy in Algeria.

The Algerian question was mooted in two French Constituent Assemblies in which Muslims sat. No basic structural changes emerged, but a general amnesty law passed which freed political prisoners who were not involved in the violence of May 1945. Ferhat Abbas brought his followers together in the UDMA (*Union Démocratique du Manifeste Algérien*) under a program which posited "a new Algeria, freely federated with a new France," and which renounced "assimilation, new masters, or separatism." Messali Hadj's new grouping, the MTLD (*Mouvement pour le triomphe des Libertés Démocratiques*) (the

[6] Julien, p. 304.

successor to the outlawed PPA), which drew heavily upon the working classes and the young intellectuals, pressed for independence. "No solution can be accepted by the Algerian people, if it does not imply an absolute guarantee of a return to our national sovereignty."

On September 20, 1947, the French National Assembly passed the so-called Algerian Statute of 1947. It was a compromise which could win a majority in the Assembly, but it pleased almost no one in Algeria. Fernand Chevalier, a colon spokesman, promised that the majority of Frenchmen in Algeria would refuse to apply it. The marvelously prophetic Félix Houphouet-Boigny, who, in 1947, represented the Ivory Coast of West Africa, put the big question.

We have, in effect, two groups of Algerians. One [MTLD] no longer believes in the French Union and demands independence. Another, the *Amis du Manifeste* and the Independent Muslims, demands a statute for an Algerian state freely associated with France.

Are you going to admit that the partisans of total independence are right by refusing the outstretched hands of the advocates of French Union? [7]

Under the Statute, Algeria was defined as a group of overseas departments. A governor general appointed by the French premier wielded executive power with the advice of a council of six. The National Assembly in Paris retained the right to apply constitutional, civil, and criminal codes in Algeria. The Algerian Assembly of 120 members, 60 from each college, functioned as an administrative institution charged with aiding the governor general to carry out policy. It voted his budget and adapted French laws to local conditions. Its first college was elected by some 464,000 Europeans and 58,000 elite Muslims who held French civic status, while the second college represented 1,400,000 Muslim electors. The Statute granted French citizenship to all inhabitants, but clearly, the Muslim elite held greater rights than their coreligionists in the second college. Muslim women remained mute and shackled by tradition, though the Statute extended them suffrage rights, which they first used in 1958. The governor general had the right to demand a second vote after twenty-four hours, on any measure, in which case a two-thirds majority became

[7] *Annales de l'Assemblée Nationale*, August 20, 1947, p. 4505.

mandatory. This meant that, in practice, the European-dominated first college held an automatic veto.

The Statute provided that in the "mixed communes" where administration was half direct and half by elected officials, Muslims should play a larger role. Ultimately "mixed communes" would evolve into "fully organized communes" which operated as the Metropolitan French counterpart.

Each of Algeria's two colleges sent fifteen representatives to the French National Assembly. These thirty men, plus the fourteen senators in the Council of the Republic and the eighteen counsellors in the Assembly of the French Union, complete Algeria's official delegation to Paris. Senators and Counsellors were elected indirectly while direct universal manhood suffrage named the thirty representatives.

The 1947 Statute failed because the colons, governor generals, and the administration in Algeria prevented its operation. Even if these people had endorsed the Statute, it still ran against the intransigent Messali Hadj who kept preaching independence and the eviction of the Europeans. The socio-economic picture favored Messali's obstructionist tactics because real wages had declined since pre-war years. Living had increased ten times above the 1938 figures while wages increased in the order of six. Ragged, ill-fed Muslims flocked to the MTLD in the municipal elections of October 1947, causing general alarm among the colons who traced this "evil" result to Muslim-loving Governor General Chataigneau.

"Chataigneau must go." And go he did, early in 1948, when Marcel-Edmond Naegelen replaced him. The new governor general, an Alsatian socialist, found the Europeans in the grip of a psychology of fear. Many apparently took seriously the Muslim slogan "la valise ou le cercueil" (the suitcase or the coffin). Officials, whose job it was to survey the Muslim population, warned Naegelen that, if nationalist propaganda circulated unchecked, the MTLD might control 90 per cent of the Muslim population. Messali Hadj's organization reached into the remote villages to win recruits, but there was no chance that the MTLD could win elections because these were carefully rigged in favor of France. Pierre Frédérix writing later in Le Monde explained the 1948 elections this way.

With the end of winter came the elections to the New Assembly created by the Statute. The government feared this creation of the French Parliament. In our three Algerian departments the choice was not between free and falsified elections. It was rather between elections rigged by the agents of Messali Hadj and elections rigged by the French administration. We chose the latter.[8]

Elections were no problem. The trouble was that the Muslim representatives had either nothing to say, or their statements bore no relationship to Muslim thinking. For six years, after the 1947 Statute, Algeria was barren of meaningful political activity. A padlock had been clamped upon the dynamic elements in all camps, so they went underground, coming up only occasionally for air. One of these moments was August 1951, when the Algerian Front for the Defense and Respect of Liberty, brought together the UDMA, the MTLD, the Algerian Communist party, and the ulemas.

This union soon dissolved. The UDMA's approach was secular, the ulema thought within Islamic reference; the MTLD endorsed direct action; the UDMA favored the dialogue with France. Finally, the MTLD and the Communists competed for support of the masses. Sometimes, however, this last pair stood together. The Algerian Communists, under the influence of their Paris comrades and Moscow, had to concern themselves with the evils of capitalistic imperialism (Soviet imperialism was fine) and the nefarious American military bases in North Africa. They were also expected to maintain solidarity in various causes, many of which they found remote or uninteresting. The MTLD was quite aware that the French Communist Party and the Communist-dominated CGT (*Confédération Générale du Travail*) trade union took no more than a casual interest in Algerian problems. Algerian workers could spear-head July 14 parades in Paris and get themselves shot or beaten up by the forces of order. When the same workers demanded the independence of Algeria, the CGT and the French Communists were very French.

Messali Hadj understood the importance of gaining an international audience. He appealed to the United Nations in 1948 and he later tried for support in anti-colonialist circles in London and New Delhi. But in May 1952, he was sent to prison in France after his supporters demonstrated in Orléansville. For a time the MTLD

[8] *Le Monde*, April 3, 1952.

reaped the harvest of its moderate rival's failure. Ferhat Abbas' vision of an autonomous republic, federated to France, disappeared in the mist of the Statute of 1947 and his UDMA lost much ground.

The MTLD might have succeeded to leadership of the nationalist movement had it not been split by quarrels between the dictatorial and old-fashioned Messali Hadj (who tried to give orders and to control the purse from his confinement in France) and the younger men in Algeria, led by Hocine Lahouel, the secretary of the central committee. By the summer of 1954, when the party split wide open, both wings stood for a militant course of action, but neither would set a deadline for an organized rebellion.

There were, however, a group of former members, all young men, who as early as 1947, split off from Messali Hadj and began to work, totally underground, toward rebellion. As early as 1947 the *Organisation Spéciale* (OS), led by Aït Ahmed, a Kabyle, began to enroll militants and to stockpile all the arms it could obtain. In April 1949 a daring hold-up (which involved Mohammed Ben Bella) of the Oran central post office netted some $9,000 for the cause. By April 1949, Ben Bella, thirty-three years old, Arab, and born at Marnia near the Moroccan frontier (four times decorated fighting with the French forces in Italy) replaced Aït Ahmed as liaison chief of the OS. Communication with the MTLD passed through Mohammed Khider, a deputy in the French National Assembly, formerly a streetcar conductor in Algiers and PPA secretary.

In 1950, when a wave of arrests jailed some of these militants, including Ben Bella, other leaders went into hiding in the Kabylia or Aurès mountains in Algeria, or took refuge in Cairo. Men like Belkacem Krim and Amar Ouamrane stayed in the mountains. Others returned to France to work for the cause with the *Fédération de France*. Khider turned up in Cairo, late in 1951, and Ben Bella and Ahmed Mahsas, who sawed their way out of prison in March 1952, were soon to reach the same destination.

A Revolution Is Organized

At Cairo in the Maghrib Office the Algerians met nationalist leaders like Allal al-Fassi from Morocco and Salah ben Youssef of the Neo-Destour. The exact relationship between Ben Bella and the Egyptian leaders is hard to discern. It seems likely that Ben Bella's stock was rising when Abdel Nasser succeeded General Naguib in 1954, possibly because of personal affinity and possibly because Nasser wanted to support a courageous Arab leader, rather than a Berber one, for the Algerian state. Khider also flourished in Cairo.

In 1954, OS leaders met frequently in Switzerland. That traditionally neutral country allowed excellent communication with the OS people in France and its meetings could not be monitored by the Egyptians. Four men dominated these clandestine planning sessions: Ben Bella, Belkacem Krim, the Kabylia leader whose job was to organize the inhabitants of those mountains, Mostefa Ben Boulaïd who did the same work in the Aurès, and Mohammed Boudiaf, a thirty-four year old intellectual and militant from the plateau area of South Constantine who had helped organize Algerians in France (1950-1953).

In March 1954, these four men enlarged their numbers to nine and formed the Revolutionary Committee for Unity and Action (*Comité Révolutionnaire d'Unité d'Action*), the CRUA. The nine were: Ben Boulaïd, Didouche, Ben M'hidi, Boudiaf, Bitat, Krim in Algeria and Ben Bella, Aït Ahmed, and Khider in Cairo. All former members of the OS, they agreed to set aside past rivalries, and through the CRUA, to organize an armed insurrection. Action, not politics, became the password, and the quadrilateral formed by Cairo, Algiers, Bern, and Paris hummed with preparations.

Militants from the OS organization in France were ordered to return to Algeria to take up the struggle. Efforts undertaken to gain the support of the faction-ridden MTLD proved unsuccessful. By July 1954, another meeting in Switzerland arranged final leadership assignments. Ben Bella, Khider, and Aït Ahmed returned to Cairo; Krim, Ben Boulaïd, and Boudiaf went back to Algeria. During the next three months the rebel organization took shape and the beginning of the uprising was scheduled. Word passed from Cairo to the mountains of Algeria that financial aid from Egypt was certain. In September, Algeria was divided into six military zones (*wilaya*), under selected local commanders. Early in October Boudiaf met *wilaya* leaders somewhere in Algeria and informed them that the rebellion would begin on November 1. Boudiaf himself left Algeria for Geneva under a fictitious name on October 27 and reached Cairo on November 2.

This planning apparently escaped French detection for the events of November 1 came clearly as a surprise. At first the extent of the rebellion was seriously underestimated. This was understandable. The explosions of a few home-made bombs, isolated sniping, the killing of seven persons, plus some property damage could not be expected to jar a French administration, supported by 50,000 troops and accustomed to spasmodic violence.

The men who planned and led the rebellion owed no debts to pre-existing political parties. Ferhat Abbas visited Cairo in July 1954, but he played no role in the uprising and his UDMA had no influence. He underestimated Algerian resistance and staying power. Otherwise he never would have continued to favor cooperation with "democratic France" after November 1954. He served a purpose in later debates in the Algerian Assembly, where speaker after speaker who had opposed the Statute of 1947 at the time, extolled its virtues once rebellion broke out.

M. Roux: "I love the Algerian Muslims. . . ."
Abbas: "Yes, like beefsteak: Bloody [saignant]. . . ."

Not until 1956, did Abbas officially join the FLN, which later became the name of the rebellious Algerian forces.

Neither the MTLD nor the Algerian Communist Party brought any serious influence to bear upon the FLN (*Front de Libération Nationale*). The former had resolutely withheld intervention; Messali Hadj liked to play the leading role and had never really accepted the CRUA's authority. Later, he actually worked with the French, and in Paris and various cities of the Metropole, his followers and the FLN members fought it out in the streets. In Algeria, too, there was fratricidal struggle. Still, many MTLD members joined the FLN. Those who stayed loyal to Messali Hadj, refused to contribute to the FLN coffers; sometimes they served in the French police force in the fifteenth *arrondissement* (the Algerian quarter in Paris) and, of course, both positions drew FLN fire.

Nor were the FLN leaders impressed with "help" from the Communist party. Members who wanted to join the FLN and fight for independence were welcomed, providing they agreed not to infiltrate or to distort the goals. When some did, they were sent on exceedingly dangerous missions from which few returned. Nationalism and international communism did not mix well.

The Algerian rebellion raised serious complications for the government of Mendès-France. Added to the existing troubles in Tunisia and Morocco, the Algerian pressure vastly increased the burden of maintaining the tricolor in the Maghrib. By November 12, the government defined its policy of "firm sanctions but no reprisal. . . ." [9] What France really had to do was to stabilize the situation in Tunisia and Morocco in order to deal with Algeria. Otherwise a general rebellion might well break out in the entire French Maghrib.

[9] Michael K. Clark, *Algeria in Turmoil, a History of the Rebellion* (New York: Praeger, 1959), p. 119. See also *Journal Officiel* for the November 12, 1954 debate.

NINE

INDEPENDENCE IN TUNISIA

AND MOROCCO, 1956

Tunisian Autonomy

In November 1954, France and Tunisia discussed a cease-fire between *fellagha* and French forces operating in.the mountains and cities. The French insisted upon peace before discussing autonomy. Standing against the success of these discussions was the Cairo pledge of 1953, taken by the nationalists of Tunisia, Morocco, and Algeria. Each group swore not to harm its Maghribi brothers in negotiating its own case with France. However, on November 22, three weeks after the outbreak of the Algerian rebellion, the Tunisians ordered the suspension of *fellagha* activity.

In retrospect, this decision appears not so much a betrayal of the Algerian and Moroccan nationalists by the Tunisians, as a failure in creative insight. Also the traditional Neo-Destour policy of moderation, dialogue, and evolution toward independence still bore weight. The Tunisian leaders were no better informed than the French on either the true strength of the FLN in 1954 or its ultimate staying power.

Negotiations between the Tunisian delegation and the representatives of France therefore continued until April 23, 1955, when a Protocol of Agreement was signed. Earlier, in February, the government of Mendès-France fell, to be succeeded by that of Edgar Faure. A jealous opposition unfairly labeled Mendès-France "the liquidator of Indo-China" and the MRP smarted under his role as "the honest broker" in the debate which ended the European Defense Community. Whisperings on the streets of Paris and in the cafés that Mendès was "not French" had sad anti-semitic overtones. The final torpedo was fired into the government by a member of his own Radical Socialist party, René Mayer of Constantine, a colon spokesman who disagreed with the North African policy. "All these slow negotiations with Tunisia are having a very bad effect on Algeria. The atmosphere in Algeria is getting worse every day." [1]

Faure, nevertheless carried though the Tunisian policy and also stuck by his predecessor's appointment of Jacques Soustelle as governor general of Algeria. Tunisia, as a result, obtained autonomy in June 1955. In theory (and largely in fact), the six conventions of June ended direct French administration. Police control, however, a keystone in the Neo-Destourian program, was to revert to the Tunisian authorities gradually over two decades. The French resident general, the supreme authority under the protectorate, gave way to a high commissioner who performed liaison between France and the Tunisian powers. Arabic became the national and official language, but French was not classified as a foreign language. France promised economic aid and support of the currency. Also France promised to provide teachers and accept Tunisians in French schools.

French inhabitants obtained better than direct proportional representation in local government and the economic chambers. Likewise, the Franco-Tunisian customs union continued and the Tunisian franc was hinged on the French equivalent.

The Tunisian delegation, Slim, Masmoudi, and Nouira, fully understood their responsibilities and realized that the basically mild Tunisian people could not resist forever. The delegation therefore made concessions to placate the colon fears. The result was an honest effort on both sides to meet future needs of both groups.

Bourguiba returned on June 1, after three years of exile, and enthusiastically endorsed the Conventions of June 3 as a step toward independence. In Cairo, however, Salah ben Youssef denounced the agreements as inadequate. Why? Probably he believed anything short

[1] Quoted by Alexander Werth, *Lost Statesman, the Strange Story of Pierre Mendès-France* (New York: Abelard-Schuman, 1958), p. 171.

of independence represented a gamble in which the odds favored France. Also in Cairo he was subject to Pan-Arabic thought and to pressure for unity of the Maghrib against the French colonizer. He wanted the Tunisians, Moroccans, and the Algerians to wage a common independence struggle. Finally, he was jealous of Bourguiba and hungry for personal power.

Autonomy thus brought internal division of the Neo-Destour Congress in November 1955; Ben Youssef lost his post as secretary general and was dropped from the party. Bourguiba was unanimously named President and Ladgham took Ben Youssef's place as secretary general. By January 1956, Ben Youssef fled to Cairo to avoid arrest. Bourguiba and Ladgham refused to serve in the government, both preferring to concentrate upon Neo-Destour affairs. The goal was still independence. When that day came, they would gladly serve.

Meanwhile the party drafted a comprehensive program of economic reform which included modernization, nationalization of *habous* lands, agricultural education plus modest plans for the beginning of processing industries and developing new sources of power.

Violence in Morocco and Independence

When Tunisia secured its autonomy, Morocco entered the throes of its most violent chapter since 1912. Each day terror and counterterror led to death. Berber tribesmen joined the protest against the dethronement; caids and pashas announced their loyalty to Sidi Mohammed. Many of these local leaders specifically denounced Al-Glawi. *Le Monde*'s reporter, as early as November 17, 1954, called this "an authentic, well-organized rebellion, a *bled es siba* of a new kind." European names began to lengthen the casualty lists. This led the colons to hire bodyguards and paid assassins, a sort of pale forerunner of the Secret Army which operated in Algeria and France in 1961-1962.

The murder of Jacques Lemaigre-Dubreil, publisher of *Maroc Presse*, a French daily in Morocco which opposed colon extremism and advocated conciliation with the Moroccans, was laid at the doorstep of European terrorists. The murdered publisher had conferred with Premier Edgar Faure twenty-four hours earlier. The first European killer arrested turned out to be Jean Delrieu, a former French police inspector who once headed the Casablanca unit against Arab terrorism.

The new Resident General, Gilbert Grandval, who had been head of the French mission in the Saar, had no love for North African colonialism or its spokesmen and profiteers. He relieved most of the old line officials and arrested some European counter-terrorists, most of whom turned out to be members of the French police. On July 14, a European mob marched upon the native quarter in Casablanca in retaliation for a bombing. Two days later the French War Veterans Association tried to prevent Grandval from entering a church. When he walked toward his car his fellow French "spat in his face, tried to manhandle him, called him 'traitor' and 'murderer.' " A few days later the colons' *Organisation de défense antiterroriste* issued a venomous brochure charging the sell-out of Morocco à la Tunisia by "the Jewish renegade Hirsch-Ollendorf, known as 'Grandval,' an accomplice of the honorable Abramovitsch, known as Mendès-France." [2]

Grandval pleaded with Faure to restore the deposed Sultan Mohammed V. But the latter apparently feared losing his majority which depended on some right-wing support, so he temporized by suggesting that the puppet Sultan, Ben Arafa, form a more representative government.

It took the events of August 20, 1955, to prove Grandval's point that the true Sultan must return. On that second anniversary of the deposition of their political and spiritual leader, the Moroccans rose in general violence and it was coordinated with the operations of the FLN on the same day in Algeria. "Tens of thousands" of Moroccan Berbers joined the fighting. Every French man, woman, and child in sight in the small town of Oued Zem, near the Middle Atlas, perished.

This time France listened and understood. Perhaps a thousand persons lost their lives in Morocco and Algeria within forty-eight hours. "A very alarmed Washington, by now thoroughly disturbed at French immobilism, urged France to please move quickly to end this situation so perilous to American air bases—and to whatever was left of the western position in North Africa." [3]

Three weeks later, President René Coty asked Ben Arafa to retire

[2] *Le Monde*, July 21, 1955, quoted by Landau, p. 371.
[3] Hahn, p. 179.

quietly to Tangier. On October 8 from Cairo Al-Fassi pledged a Maghrib Liberation Army of Moroccan and Algerian freedom fighters under the command of Ben Bella. This force, he claimed, would place Mohammed V on his rightful throne. By the end of October, Sidi Mohammed reached Nice from Madagascar and went to Paris for a round of ornate receptions and honors. Al-Glawi went to Paris where, in the Sultan's hotel, the Henry IV, he begged forgiveness from the wronged monarch.

On November 17, 1955, the Sultan Sidi Mohammed ben Youssef, Mohammed V, returned to Morocco, and on the following day made a speech from the throne which outlined his future course. On this twenty-eighth anniversary of his accession he told of forthcoming negotiations with the French government. "We rejoice in being able to announce the end of the regime of trusteeship and of the protectorate and the coming of an era of freedom and independence." He promised a new Morocco, "an emancipation of the individual," and a continuation of friendship with France. He saw ahead three immediate tasks:

(1) The administration of public affairs.

(2) The creation of democratic institutions resulting from free elections and founded on the principle of separation of powers, within the framework of a constitutional monarchy granting to Moroccans of all faiths citizenship rights and the exercise of political and trade union freedom. It stands to reason that Moroccan Jews have the same rights and duties as other Moroccans.

(3) The third task of the future Moroccan government will be to open negotiations with the French government on the basis of . . . the ideas of freedom and democracy. . . . The Moroccan government . . . must define . . . the real meaning of the independence of our country and the new relations of interdependence between France and Morocco on the basis of their equality and with mutual respect for each other's sovereignty.[4]

Once Mohammed V returned to his throne, the next demand was obvious: independence. In this there was no problem of national unity, but Istiqlal's predominant position threatened the Sultan's

[4] Text from Landau, Appendix X, pp. 397-399.

freedom of action. In other words, the Sultan did not wish to see one political party or any personality place the throne in the shade. This situation helps to explain why the later independent Morocco never yielded to a one-party system.

In appointing a government, Mohammed V cleverly divided the posts between parties, giving Istiqlal the lion's share. Si Bekkai, a member of the Popular Independent Party, became premier. Still Istiqlal obtained seven of fifteen cabinet posts; the PDI (*Parti Démocratique d'Indépendence*) received four; and the independents got the rest. Lyazidi became minister of commerce and industry. Leaders like Al-Fassi and Balafrej, and like Bourguiba in Tunisia, preferred to delay their service in the ministry until independence.

During February and March 1956, talks moved forward with France despite the fact that some disorders continued, and General Franco held up an obstructive hand. Fighting between the French Foreign Legion and the Moroccan Liberation Army was at least organized fighting, and in this respect an improvement over terror and counter-terror. All Moroccans wanted not simply independence, but also territorial integrity which meant that Spanish Morocco and Tangier were within their sights. General Franco showed no inclination to cooperate and he further opposed loosening the Spanish administrative grip in Tetuán.

What really mattered was the serious purpose of the Moroccan Sultan and the Mollet government in Paris, to reach an agreement. France was intent upon simplifying her North African problems, and Mollet, after being pelted by ripe tomatoes, other vegetables, and even rocks by the Europeans when he visited Algiers on February 6, fully understood the importance of peace and friendship between France and Morocco. He, therefore, instructed his foreign minister, Christian Pineau, to move rapidly toward an accord with the Sultan's delegates.

The Declaration of La Celle-St. Cloud of November 6, 1955, was signed by Pineau and Si Bekkai on March 2, 1956. The two governments agreed,

That the Treaty of Fez of March 30, 1912, no longer corresponds to the demands of modern life and can no longer govern Franco-Moroccan relations. Consequently the Government of the French Republic solemnly confirms the recognition of the independence of Morocco, which particularly implies a diplomacy and an army, as well as its willingness to respect and to make respected the integrity of Moroccan territory guaranteed by international treaty. The Government of the French Republic and his majesty Mohammed V, Sultan of Morocco, declare that the negotiations which just opened in Paris between Morocco and France, as sovereign and equal states, have for their objective the conclusion of new accords which will define the interdependence of the two countries in domains where their interests are common, which will organize their cooperation on a basis of liberty and equality, notably in matters of defense, external relations, economy, and culture, and which will guarantee the rights and liberties of the French living in Morocco and the Moroccans living in France, with full respect for the sovereignty of the two states.[5]

Accompanying this declaration was a protocol which placed Morocco within the franc zone, regulated status of French civil servants working in Morocco, and changed the title (and function) of the resident general to high commissioner.

The settlement with France placed the spotlight upon relations between Morocco and Spain. On April 7, 1956, the Spanish protectorate ended officially when a joint declaration was signed in Madrid. The following October 29, the eight power international administration in Tangier handed authority to the Sultan. With the exception of the *presidios* of Ceuta and Melilla on the Mediterranean coast, the Ifni enclave on the Atlantic, Spanish Saharan areas, and Mauretania in the far south, future targets for Moroccan nationalists, territorial integrity came in the independence package.

By 1956 Moroccan nationalism was twenty-five years old. Its leaders had matured in the ways of politics and administrative know-how. At home they made the urban masses politically conscious while abroad they learned to handle their cause in the world's capitals—Cairo, Paris, Madrid, Washington and New York. Increasingly, after 1951, the Berbers of central Morocco, the Rif, and the Middle Atlas threw their weight behind the independence movement.

The vital role was the Sultan's. Mohammed V grew with his tasks to emerge, in 1956, as one of the statesmen of the Third World. He

[5] Text reproduced by Roger le Tourneau, *Évolution politique de l'Afrique du Nord musulmane, 1920-1961* (Paris: Colin, 1962), p. 249, from *Le Monde*, March 4-5, 1956 and *Revue de Presse*, No. 4 (April 1956).

developed a sensitive control over events and situations without which the nationalist movement might well have degenerated into disorder and chaos. At the same time he symbolized both the Moroccan state and, true to Islamic practice, he led the faithful. Returning to his throne, the "Beloved Sultan" set aside the revenge and rancor which men of smaller stature might have invoked. Al-Glawi's treachery was relegated to the forgotten past. In a similar vein, he understood that the well-being of his people depended upon cordial relationship with France and with the world. The trying adjustments which lay ahead required all this good resolution and more.

Tunisian Independence

Tunisia, whose Neo-Destour was more highly developed and organized than Istiqlal, and which always prided itself on advancement over its neighbors, lagged behind Morocco in gaining independence. In early 1956 Tunisian leaders knew the Declaration of La Celle-St. Cloud would soon lead to Morocco's independence. Ben Youssef, who preached Arabism and integral independence for the entire Maghrib, and who had unsuccessfully tried to displace Bourguiba from leadership of the Neo-Destour, had fled to Cairo. But the plots of his followers lingered on. The time was ripe to extract the same claims which France conceded Morocco.

Three circumstances led France to agree on March 20, 1956, that Tunisian autonomy was inadequate, that independence à la Maroc was necessary. One related to the Bey who, according to French High Commissioner Roger Seydoux, asked that France remain. This was true; the Bey's personal comforts were secure under the French. Ladgham, one of the Tunisian negotiators with France, soon blocked this pretense by obtaining a written request, from the Bey, for the end of the Bardo Treaty.

A second force favoring independence was the first national elections in Tunisia, scheduled for the spring. A Constituent Assembly elected by the people would be able to speak in the name of the nation. It surely would press the country's case with France.

Early in February 1956, Bourguiba entered into long informal discussions with French representatives, and, on leap year day, the Tunisian delegation of Ben Ammar, Ladgham, Slim, and Masmoudi opened official talks which they hoped would scrap the Bardo Treaty and lead to independence. At first the French concessions were small —Tunisia might have a miniature army and diplomatic corps but no true independence. On March 9, a violent mob of colons protested the murder of two French farmers by Youssefists, and they wrecked the American Consulate and the USIS library in Tunis. The root of all evil, in the colon mind, was American influence. The French were in no hurry to stop the damage or to arrest the mob which shouted "Down with América, Down with Mendès-France, Down with the Jews!" This scandalous behavior furnished the Tunisians with another set of favorable circumstances.

With the Algerian rebellion daily gaining momentum and the colons in Tunis insulting the keystone of NATO, the French negotiators may well have softened. In any case, after refusing independence on March 17, Foreign Minister Pineau was bluntly told by Ladgham that if France could not go all the way, then the Constituent Assembly in Tunisia would proclaim independence. Bourguiba met twice with Pineau that evening and France finally agreed to scrap the Bardo Treaty. Three days later, a protocol, similar in terms to that received by Morocco, was signed. Details of the change were to be ironed out later. The impatient Tunisian government, without even waiting for the French ratification, assumed independence and France made no serious protest.

There was no denying that once the nationalists in the three French Maghribi states moved from speech-making and the publication of tracts into organized action, which included boycott, violence, and all-out rebellion, as in Algeria, the days of the old system were numbered. Doubtless, France could have held out longer and possibly even temporarily crushed opposition in Tunisia. In Morocco, once the Berbers joined the independence march, agitating side by side with the Arabs, a very large force would have been required to hold the protectorate. In retrospect, the Berber *Dahir* of 1930 and the dethronement of Mohammed V were unnecessary blunders. These acts hastened independence. The Algerian rebellion certainly shortened the battle in Morocco and Tunisia. And by the same token, after March 1956, France was in a better position to concentrate her undivided attention upon Algeria.

In all three areas, the colons vitiated constructive efforts from Metropolitan France to engineer evolutionary change. In Algeria, the French inhabitants were more numerous, as time went on, more fanatical, and more bitter and frightened after they studied the recent past in Morocco and Tunisia. "Algeria is France," they stubbornly said. For awhile this became bitterly true.

TEN

The Algerian Revolution

1954-1962

No people seeking independence in the post World War II period underwent a more difficult or demoralizing ordeal than the Algerians. By the time the cease-fire was called in March 1962, the Algerians counted one million dead, two million in regroupment camps inside the country, 300,000 refugees in Morocco, Tunisia, and Libya, and 150,000 persons in and out of *camps d'hébérgement* (reformation or brain-washing centers). When one estimates the total Muslim population in 1954 at nine or ten million inhabitants, the human costs of independence loom incredibly high. France, too, paid an inordinate price in men and money in Algeria, to say nothing of the French conscience. And in May 1958, the Algerian war led directly to the collapse of the Fourth Republic and the installation of General Charles de Gaulle's Fifth Republic, the full effects of which can scarcely yet be measured.

For a number of years the Algerian question became a permanent item on the UN agenda where agonized delegates, friends and foes of France and the Algerians—it did not matter—all hoped that some way, somehow, the killing and destruction could end. Algerian spokesmen toured the world stating the nationalist case while, in the same world, official French representatives argued that Algeria was a domestic French problem and would eventually be solved as such. Robert Lacoste, who became Governor General in February 1956, spoke of the "last quarter hour" of the struggle. This estimate missed the target by six years minus fifteen minutes.

The Algerian problem weakened the NATO shield when France detached troops from Germany and shipped them across to North Africa. The French fleet, too, was pulled out and sent to the Mediterranean to blockade the "French" coast of Algeria. The rebellion worked a great hardship upon France's allies, who disliked exposing themselves to the loss of good will in the entire Third World, to say nothing of important parts of the free world. But the greatest burden, by far, fell upon the people of Algeria.

The first twenty months of the struggle, from the November outbreak in 1954, to the Soummam Valley Congress of the FLN in August 1956, represent a time of organization, trial and error, and some disunity with the Algerian camp.

French forces in Algeria, which numbered approximately 50,000 men in November 1954, were increased to 250,000 by May 1956. By the sixth year of the war, a half-million French soldiers were deployed in Algeria. Costs mounted to a billion dollars a year. Against this force, equipped with the finest military hardware NATO could provide (helicopters were particularly useful in ferreting out the Algerian Freedom Fighters who operated in small groups in places where nature provided excellent cover) the Algerians began, with very few men and little more than hunting weapons and home-made bombs. By August 1956, the ALN (*Armée de Libération Nationale*), boasted a fairly efficient structure. Also, throughout the war, improved weapons reached the Freedom Fighters. They were purchased abroad or donated by friendly Arab states (like Egypt) and reached Algeria via various routes, including camel caravans which ran from southern Morocco, westward into the Algerian Sahara, thence northward, to supply the *wilayas*, or military zones. Some weapons were captured from the French.

In the early phase, hit-and-run guerrilla tactics characterized Freedom Fighter action. Later, organized battles, sometimes coordinated with outside pressure upon the French (as in the Morocco uprising of August 20, 1955), involved units in company strength. The ALN ultimately became an efficient fighting force of 60,000 men with an almost unlimited backstop of eager Algerian men and women.

The FLN did not begin from scratch in organizing the Muslim population behind the independence banner. The older PPA–MTLD armature, whose basic unit was the fluid cell, served a new master, with the OS and the CRUA making liaison. The rugged terrain and the hospitality of the population favored the Freedom Fighters. French forces, even when they reached a half-million men, found 850,000 square miles of Algeria an impossibly large area to pacify. Thus, considerable initiative rested with the ALN. It could choose the *wilaya*, in which heavy action would be waged, at the same time preparing other sectors for future action and assigning still other *wilayas* as rest zones. In the remote areas of the Aurès and in the Kabylia mountains, pacification in any permanent sense proved unattainable.

Expansion of the FLN

In 1956, the FLN broadened its base notably. In the spring, Ferhat Abbas and Dr. Ahmed Francis, his brother-in-law, both reached Cairo where they could freely acknowledge their allegiance. Ulema leaders like Tewfik al Madani did the same thing. These new recruits secured the support of the bourgeois UDMA and the religious elite. In March 1956, the FLN organized a trade union, the UGTA (*Union Générale des Travailleurs Algériens*) to compete against Messali Hadj's USTA (*Union Syndicale des Travailleurs Algériens*), formed the previous month in Paris. The UGTA secured the backing of the International Confederation of Trade Unions by July of the same year. This affiliation became extremely useful since it provided an international platform for Algerian nationalism. In a country like the United States, George Meany, president of the AFL–CIO, spoke in favor of the Algerian cause before the American Legion National Convention in September. "We of the AFL–CIO protest vigorously against even a single American helicopter or any other military equipment designated for the North Atlantic Treaty Organization and the defense of free Europe, being used against the Algerian national liberation forces." [1]

In August 1956, the FLN held its first congress in the Soummam Valley in Kabylia. At this meeting, which external leaders such as Ben Bella were unable to attend because of short notice and danger-

[1] *The New York Times*, September 5, 1956.

ous transportation problems, the "internals" who were mostly Kabyles dominated. This predominance of internal Berber chieftains over the men who worked from the outside, led to the first outward tensions between the two groups.

At Soummam Valley, the ALN underwent structural organization which lasted, with few changes, until the revolution's end. The CNRA (National Council of the Algerian Revolution), composed of seventeen men and seventeen substitutes, became the Front's highest authority, a kind of legislature which passed on all major decisions. The original seventeen included the historic chiefs, Ben Bella, Aït Ahmed, Boudiaf, Bitat, Khider, Ben Boulaïd (who was killed early in the revolution), and *wilaya* leaders such as Ben M'hidi and Belkacem Krim plus recently affiliated political leaders such as Ferhat Abbas and Tewfik al Madani. Some *wilaya* leaders were on the alternate list.

In addition, a streamlined executive of five men, called the Committee of Coordination and Execution, selected from CNRA members serving inside Algeria, took shape at Soummam. Two of the five met early death but three of the CCE (Krim, Khedda, and Dahlab) served in the later Provisional Government of the Algerian Revolution which was organized in September 1958.

The Soummam declaration placed political aims above military ends, and recognized the primacy of the internal Freedom Fighters over the externals. All its structural decisions supported the idea of collective leadership. A military statute regulated army pay and planned a host of auxiliary services. The ALN became practically a state in itself with its concern for labor unions, education, widows and orphans, its propaganda and information service, a psychological warfare branch, and, of course, a logistics section. Women were brought into the ALN and the Front in various functions—as nurses, teachers, propagandists, messengers, auxiliary fighters, and even weapon's porters or bomb-throwers.

By 1957, reliable newspaper reporters who observed the ALN remarked on its discipline and organization. Thomas Hodgkin caught the deep implications when he wrote in the *Manchester Guardian* (July 13, 1957):

Following the classic pattern of revolutionary wars, what has come into being during these last three years is not simply a new kind of army but also the rudiments of a new form of State—with its clandestine (or semi-clandestine) local authorities, courts of justice, police, schools, medical services, communications, and taxation.

Meetings of the CNRA took place roughly each year, and that body, in March 1962, ratified the final Evian accords with France. In 1957, at Cairo, the CNRA was enlarged to fifty-four members and the CCE to nine. The following year, on September 19, after de Gaulle came to power in France and a new approach to peace seemed in the offing, the Provisional Government of the Algerian Republic, with Ferhat Abbas as prime minister and the imprisoned Ben Bella as first deputy prime minister, was announced from Cairo, Tunis, and Rabat. In December 1959, the third CNRA meeting, held in Tripoli, acknowledged that future independent Algeria would, under conditions of universal suffrage, ratify or veto the provisory decisions taken by this body. CNRA decisions required a two-thirds majority, and it was said that on final negotiations with France a four-fifths rule would prevail. These meetings, always held in utmost secrecy, and with a secret membership, made the highest decisions.

Before de Gaulle's Fifth Republic took shape, in 1958, the French weakened the FLN's external leadership, but never really brought the ALN to heel. Four leaders were arrested in October 1956, when French ground authorities persuaded a French pilot of a commercial plane belonging to Air Maroc to land at Algiers instead of Tunis. Passengers Ben Bella, Bitat, Khider, and Aït Ahmed, flying under Moroccan safe-conduct promises, fell into French hands. Sultan Mohammed V, host of these FLN leaders, was furious and, considering that the hospitality of his household had been violated, offered to give his son as hostage for the kidnapped FLN ministers. Protest resignations took place within the French cabinet and civil administration by persons who wanted no part in this kidnapping. Tactically it was reminiscent of the deposing of Mohammed V, and politically, it proved to be almost as great a blunder. In Meknès a Moroccan retaliation took fifty European lives.

The next month, the Suez invasion, largely motivated in the French case to check Egypt's aid to the FLN, met with quick disaster when the United States and the Soviet Union together flashed red lights.

In 1957, the winds from Algeria carried new straws. The nature of the nationalist rebellion and the French counteraction underwent change. Each side faced a new set of problems and the international community, more keenly aware of the issues, eagerly watched the unfolding events. Germaine Tillion, the French anthropologist and Algerian authority, returned to that country in June 1957, as a member of the International Committee Against the Regime of Concentration Camps. She returned home convinced that Algerian resistance could not be crushed. "It now seemed to me that as soon as the (ALN) military machine would be reduced these underground political forms would reconstitute themselves." [2]

In Morocco and Tunisia, the Algerian rebellion attracted great sympathy and a large amount of public and private help, which took various forms. This posture led inevitably to deteriorating relationships between these countries and the former protector. It also, of course, weakened the day-to-day rapport between the French who stayed in these countries after independence as teachers, technicians, businessmen, and administrators, and the nationals. So, for these neighboring Arab countries, the Algerian rebellion, which they instinctively supported, automatically inflicted the cost of reduced French aid, and at times exposed them to French military reprisals as in the bombing of Sakiet Sidi Youssef in Tunisia in 1958. The immediate future of Morocco and Tunisia depended intimately upon the outcome of the Algerian question.

As the tempo of the Algerian rebellion and the French repression increased, large numbers of Muslim refugees flowed into Tunisia and Morocco. By 1960 each neighbor harbored approximately 150,000 refugees. This situation placed Morocco and Tunisia between various international, private, and public welfare organizations, the Algerian refugees, and their Provisional Government of the Algerian Republic. Inevitably, this led to strain.

So did the fact that units of the Algerian Liberation Army were based in and supplied from Morocco and Tunisia. When these Algerian soldiers practised demolition on Tunisian power lines, the latter government naturally protested vehemently. Despite these difficulties both Tunisia and Morocco supported the rebellion but these states breathed a sigh of relief when it ended.

[2] "Le récit de Germaine Tillion," *L'Express*, August 28, 1958.

In 1957, increased evidence of the use of torture by French forces in Algeria piled up in Paris, where it caused considerable protest and soul-searching. Brisk letters and petitions decrying these practices signed by extremely distinguished Frenchmen, reached the desk of the President of the Republic. In Algiers someone fired a bazooka shell into the office of the French Commander in Chief, General Raoul Salan, and it clearly was no Muslim.

On July 2, Democratic Senator John F. Kennedy introduced a resolution asking President Eisenhower and Secretary of State Dulles to use American influence, either through NATO or the good offices of Bourguiba and Mohammed V, "to achieve a solution which [would] recognize the independent personality of Algeria and establish the basis for a settlement interdependent with France and the neighboring nations." [3] Nothing came of the Kennedy resolution, but the Algerian nationalists always remembered it favorably, and official and colonial France, of course, detested it.

The Beginning of the End of the Fourth Republic

By 1958 a new *loi-cadre* for Algeria finally passed the French National Assembly, but remained largely a dead letter because events in North Africa brought about the collapse of the Fourth Republic before the summer. The direct line between the Algerian rebellion and the death of the Fourth began one hour before noon, on February 8, 1958. At that moment eleven French B-26 bombers and six escort planes bombed the Tunisian village of Sakiet Sidi Youssef, killing sixty-nine persons, twenty-one of whom were children. This action brought to a violent culmination a series of border incidents along the Algerian-Tunisian line where French troops and Freedom Fighters faced one another. A week later, France and Tunisia accepted "good offices" of the United States and the United Kingdom. By April 15, the National Assembly abandoned the "good offices" approach and Premier Gaillard resigned. Voting against the Anglo-American mediation were the French moderates and Communists with the strong assist of the "four paragons of French Algeria": Soustelle, Duchet, Bidault, and Morice. This opened a protracted crisis which led de

[3] *Congressional Record*, Vol. 103, Part 8, 85th Congress, First Session, July 2, 1957, p. 10780.

Gaulle back to power under the prearranged umbrella of the French army.

Throughout 1957 and 1958, the FLN kept the pressure on in the mountains and cities; at the same time it tried to intensify the internationalization of its cause. Arms procurement problems were largely solved, but, since these weapons often originated in Communist countrics, Morocco and Tunisia, whose ports accepted these shipments when they got through the French blockade, faced embarrassment in their relations with France and the West. These neighboring Arab states also feared a preponderance of Cairo's influence in high Algerian councils. In December 1957, FLN representatives sat in an Afro-Asian conference in Cairo where Soviet delegates were present. Possibly this added up to no more than the fact that the FLN would accept all the help anyone would offer. Bourguiba and Mohammed V, who both believed in solidarity of the Maghrib, called a conference at Tangier to define the common interest of Morocco, Tunisia, and Algeria. Ferhat Abbas, Abdel Hamid Mehri, Mohammed Boumendjel, and Abdelhafid Boussouf composed the Algerian delegation. All later sat in the GPRA and Boumendjel, called "Boom" by his friends, survived all the political ups and downs and sat in Ben Bella's cabinets when independence came.

At the Tangier conference, the three parties concerned proclaimed the "right of the Algerian people to sovereignty and independence" as the sole condition for peace. The communiqué also noted the desire to create a future Maghrib federation. More important than these words was the successful patching up of outstanding difficulties between the FLN and Morocco. The conference also denounced the West for supporting French colonialism. Writing later, Mahmoud Chérif, a member of the FLN's Committee of Coordinations and Execution, considered the conference to be a turning point in the war because it built a united North African front, something France had desperately tried to prevent.[4]

Another African conference, this one held at Accra in Ghana, April 20-28, 1958, attended by Morocco, Tunisia, Libya, Sudan, Liberia, Ghana, Ethiopia, and the United Arab Republic broke several lances

---

[4] Charles-Henri Favrod, La Révolution Algérienne (Paris: Plon, 1959), pp. 214-215.

for Algerian independence. These countries agreed to give the Algerians material help, to ask the French to negotiate a political withdrawal from Algeria, and to recognize the FLN as the nation's spokesman. A permanent traveling commission was created with the mission of explaining the Algerian case to the world. On October 18, the Council of the Arab League assessed its members $34,400,000 for the support of the Algerian revolution. By way of comparison, it is interesting to note that in the previous January France obtained $655,-000,000 from the European Payments Union, International Monetary Fund, and the United States.

De Gaulle Intervenes

The events in Algiers and Paris, beginning on May 13, 1958, vitally influenced the future course of the Algerian Revolution and the entire French policy. It brought to the French political stage old faces in new costumes. Premier Gaillard resigned on April 15 and not until nearly a month later did it appear that Pierre Pflimlin would succeed him. In Algeria, the reaction of the French army command and the colon leaders to Pflimlin's investiture was militantly thumbs down. European activists demonstrated, the army took over control in Algiers (through a Committee of Public Safety), and finally, through threats to drop parachutists upon Paris plus well-organized assistance from supporters of General Charles de Gaulle (if not the general himself), succeeded in bringing down the Fourth Republic. Thus, de Gaulle again entered the Algerian question officially. He came to Algiers and told the assembled multitude (who brought no tomatoes this time) and the disobedient French army that he "understood them." They cheered wildly, not really knowing what he meant but reading into the statement that he stood for French Algeria forever.

He moved quickly to bring about peace on his terms by suggesting that the "rebels" needed only to raise the white flag to meet with French negotiation. At the same time he ordered a heavy military offensive under General Maurice Challe, and the tightening of the Challe-Morice electrified barriers which the French had built on Algeria's east and west borders to prevent the flow of supplies and men from Tunisia and Morocco. The GPRA, formed in September, refused the white flag offer, considering it a surrender rather than a truce symbol. But de Gaulle in October 1958, came up with the Constantine Plan, in an attempt to ameliorate life for the indigenous Algerians within a five-year period. Salaries and wages were to be raised to a level comparable to those in Metropolitan France; 617,500 acres were to be distributed to Muslim farmers; the oil and natural gas of the Sahara were to be tapped and distributed; a great metallurgical and chemical industry would take shape; housing for a million people constructed; additional regular employment for 400,000 workers would result from the plan; and two-thirds of the Muslim children of school age would have classrooms and teachers.

All this did not come to pass by 1962 when independence came, but important beginnings had been made and some educational facilities were built. The ALN never tried to sabotage any of these installations since sooner or later they would belong to independent Algeria. The Secret Army of European activists reacted in opposite fashion. By the end of 1961 and throughout the first six months of 1962, particularly from March to June (the period between cease-fire and the vote for independence), the Secret Army did its best to destroy any facility the future Algerian state might inherit from the French presence.

Again, in January 1959, after the UN had voted the previous month by a 35 to 18 majority to recognize "the right of the Algerian people to independence" and recommended "negotiations between the two interested parties," de Gaulle spoke of an honorable peace. The time was still too early for a full-hearted accommodation between France and the FLN through its Provisional Government of the Algerian Republic.

But 1959 witnessed important progress. Six new African nations quickly extended recognition to the GPRA, thereby joining the Afro-Asian states which had already taken that step. The Chinese People's Republic had been among the first to grant de jure recognition, while the Soviet Union (where the revolution was middle-aged), whose leaders enjoyed the sight of 500,000 French troops in Algeria rather than Germany, moved slowly to a de facto appreciation of the GPRA.

De Gaulle made the important news of that year when in his September speech he recognized Algeria's right to self-determination and then quickly exposed the possibilities. There could be integration (gallicization), which the colons and the high French army brass in

Algeria loved, or association, which de Gaulle himself favored, or secession, which might please the FLN but would lead to catastrophe for the Algerian people, according to the general. It was an extremely comprehensive proposition calculated to start the thought process of the various factions; it was carefully hedged. Peace must prevail first, then elections, and de Gaulle himself would choose the time. "Only thus could public opinion in France and nationalist sentiments in Algeria be reconciled, and only thus today (1963) can various necessary fictions in Franco-Algerian relations be maintained." [5]

Self-determination was a principal which no upstanding colon or "poor-white" of Algeria could concede. Neither could Jacques Soustelle or Georges Bidault or other partisans of integration, including high-ranking French officers of North African birth such as Marshal Juin. So, in January 1960, up went the barricades in Algiers, and Pierre Lagaillarde, the French student leader, and Joseph Ortiz, the barkeep, harangued their "troops." The French army did not move to break up this phalanx of dead-enders for French Algeria, until de Gaulle ordered and ordered again. Then, slowly, the great beast did a reluctant job and the European insurgents went home amidst cheers from the French community. Leaders were hailed before French tribunals or ran away. In all this, the Muslims stood moot and the GPRA favored de Gaulle over Lagaillarde or Ortiz.

In June, de Gaulle proceeded with the staging. This time he summoned FLN delegates to Melun and then brushed them off like moths in his dress uniform. Melun resembled a softening-up game played against the FLN and French political opponents of the Gaullist doctrine.

De Gaulle kept demanding a cease-fire before serious talks could be held. The FLN felt that no acceptable decisions could be reached unless the fighting continued. By January 1961, de Gaulle obtained a 75 per cent majority in France in a referendum on his self-determination policy. In Algeria 69 per cent voted favorably.

New talks were scheduled for April between de Gaulle's representatives and the Algerians. These were postponed when French spokesmen announced they would consult "all tendencies" in Algeria, attempting

[5] Charles F. Gallagher, *The United States and North Africa* (Cambridge, Mass.: Harvard, 1963), p. 112.

to play on the old Arab-Berber schism, a course the GPRA ignored, insisting it was the sole spokesman of the nation. Messali Hadj could have no part in a revolution he was not fighting, nor could the Arab-Berber split be brought to the surface at this point. Later it would return on its own terms.

Reaction and Success

The next act belonged to four French generals who felt that de Gaulle had betrayed the army and the French in Algeria in nine different ways. He had said he "understood" them; he promised never to negotiate with the FLN, and he insisted upon a cease-fire before any talks. In fairness, de Gaulle made these promises but he also offered self-determination, shied away from "integration," and the electorates overwhelmingly supported him. When, in frustration at the GPRA's equally frustrated reaction to the "all tendencies" approach, de Gaulle spoke vaguely of regrouping the people of Algeria who wanted French protection into a coastal zone, he triggered a military uprising.

This time Generals Salan, Challe, Jouhaud, and Zeller plus a batch of colonels who despised the Fourth and Fifth Republic's treatment of the army, the imminent end of the Foreign Legion, and self-determination, as well as de Gaulle's broken word, resolved to do something about it. At his trial, Major Denoix de Saint-Marc explained his motivation eloquently and honestly.

> You can ask a soldier to die—that is his job—but not to lie, to cheat, and to perjure himself. I have been fighting for France for fifteen years. I have seen my *légionnaires* die for France, though foreigners by blood, they are Frenchmen by the blood they have spilt. My choice was for them.[6]

Despite the support of several crack regiments, the Four Generals' Rebellion failed within a few days; not, however, before a very nervous Premier Michel Debré asked Parisians to go out on the streets and "dissuade the paratroopers from their heavy enterprises." Paris feared another May 13 and an assault upon the regime, this time the Fifth Republic. The four generals and their colonels and majors failed because they did not apply the methods of the "new warfare" properly.

[6] Quoted by Dorothy Pickles, *Algeria and France from Colonialism to Cooperation* (New York: Praeger, 1963), p. 85.

They found themselves helpless without the conscripts and the people, which their text-book writer Mao Tse-tung said they must move among, "as the fish in the water." The generals never had enough support on their side either in Algeria, where repression influenced the Muslims more than good works and where the European activists and army professional could not see eye to eye, or in France where the nation rallied to de Gaulle.

In the midst of the crisis, the GPRA announced that for once, all sensible Frenchmen and the FLN were in complete agreement. Better de Gaulle than Salan. So de Gaulle won again and a *rapprochement* with the FLN appeared much more imminent when the uprising was quelled. One saddening result, however, was that high-ranking French officers and some men deserted to the Secret Army Organization. From this point until July 1962, when Algeria secured its independence, the OAS worked to destroy life and property of its opponents and to sabotage the Franco-Algerian peace negotiations.

These, however, were still far from fulfillment. Negotiators, meeting at Evian in May and June, failed to agree upon the prerequisites for a referendum, nor could the disposition of the Algerian Sahara with its newly-found riches be decided. In July, another series of meetings at Lugrin accomplished almost nothing. The Sahara was the key: the FLN claimed sovereignty, the French wanted its wealth which they had prospected and developed.

After the collapse of negotiations at Evian and Lugrin (August 1961), the CNRA named Youssef ben Khedda as premier of the Provisional Government in place of Ferhat Abbas. Ben Khedda, who earlier held command in the Algiers *wilaya* as a member of the Committee of Coordination and Execution, held close ties with the Army of National Liberation. Unlike Abbas, a French-trained moderate, the new premier was a militant. The FLN thus served notice that it would continue the rebellion; even enlarge its scope, if necessary, by calling for more active help from its support in the "Third World," particularly Communist China. At the same time, it would negotiate with France but would not depart from the basic goals of the revolution: independence and territorial integrity. The Algerian Sahara could not be sacrificed for peace. *Le Monde* cryptically remarked that a sixty-year-old Girondist stepped down in favor of a forty-year-old Montagnard.

In October 1961, de Gaulle admitted that the disputed portion of the Sahara belonged to Algeria. This conciliatory statement, made at a time when the OAS was doing its best to assassinate de Gaulle, paved the way for the final negotiations which began again at Evian on March 7, 1962. Eleven days later a cease-fire was reached, and, on the 19th of March, it went into effect. These Evian accords received the overwhelming support of the voters of Metropolitan France and Algeria. In France on April 8, though 24 per cent of the electorate abstained, 91 per cent voted to endorse the agreement. In Algeria, on the following July 1, abstentions were no more than 8 per cent, and 99.72 of the votes cast favored independence.

The end of the Franco-Algerian ordeal came swiftly once the French army, the colons, and the various activist European organizations in Algeria were cut down to size. The Secret Army did its dirtiest work between Evian and Independence Day in Algeria. These diehards took pleasure in shooting down Muslims on the streets, in entering classrooms and killing European and Muslim teachers in front of their pupils. They raided hospitals at gun point and liquidated patients in their beds. One day they charged a truck with high explosives and sent it rolling down the hill to explode among Muslim dockers who waited for work, killing some 120. They set fire to the library of the University of Algiers and burned a half-million books. Their purpose was to kill and destroy and, if possible, to goad the Muslims into counterattack in which case the French inhabitants could call upon the French army to save them from a *jihad* or holy war. But the *jihad* seemed to be on the Christian side; the Muslims showed an unbelievable discipline. They could afford to wait the last quarter of an hour, for a million Muslims were already dead. At the end, when the OAS faced armed men instead of sitting ducks, they ran away. Charles Gallagher put the case brilliantly when he remarked, "the only fitting epitaph for this ending was that the colonial period died as it had lived, in violence and incomprehension." [7]

The entire world breathed a tremendous sigh of relief as France

[7] *Op. cit.*, p. 115.

cut off a cancerous limb. Independent Algeria was born in great travail, and yet, for this state and the rest of the Maghrib, the stage of
development which was to follow would call upon a different kind
of courage, sacrifice, even intelligence. It was a period which would
surely consume the creative energies and devotion of still another
generation.

ELEVEN

NORTHWEST AFRICA TODAY

In searching for an understanding of former French Northwest Africa we must consider three major influences upon its history. These states were predominantly marked by their Muslim background. Islam and the Arabic language have influenced and shaped the way the people believe, think, and act. A second basic molding force is the area's recent past, which lay within the French empire. Despite the sharp political changes of the last years—the achieving of independence—the three states clearly bear the imprint of French civilization and culture. In all probability, it will be the French language which the Maghrib will use to unlock the secrets of modern technology and science, even if Arabic remains the language of the indigenous culture and the official language according to the new constitutions.

The third major influence upon these states stems from the nationalist movements and the traumatic conditions under which independence was attained. Nationalism is definitely in the saddle, a western import, grafted upon an ancient land. Its thrust obtained independence, at present the most respected commodity in these countries.

Within Morocco, Algeria, and Tunisia there are varied reactions to these common forces. Morocco and Tunisia never felt the French imprint as deeply as Algeria. No one, not even the proudest colon, ever claimed that Morocco or Tunisia *was* France. Morocco had a long kingly tradition, close ties to Spain, and relative isolation from the outer world. Neither Morocco nor Tunisia paid anything like the price paid by Algeria for independence. In that troubled state the seven and a half year rebellion, with its attending death, destruction, and legacy of hate, engendered a unique environment.

Algeria's leaders were revolutionaries, men of action. They moved quickly from the first phase, the struggle for independence, into the stage of socialist development, but were faced with frightful handicaps —many of them, products of the struggle itself. When the population of a country has been decimated and when another 20 per cent suffered years of idleness and starvation in forced detention, and when the productive dynamic (European) minority has for one reason or another left the scene, then the transition from colony to independence, from war to peace, from fighting to producing, is one which requires not only the utmost sacrifice, but also, time, maturity, and trained human resources; and these are exactly the elements in short supply.

Some observers characterize Algeria's first year of independence as "catastrophic." And no doubt from a certain European viewpoint, it was exactly that. But then, for great numbers of Muslims, life had been catastrophic for a very long time. The great difference after July 3, 1962 (independence day in Algeria), was that the indigenous Arabo-Berber people, and anyone else who wanted to risk becoming an Algerian (and a few Europeans did) had the right and duty to prescribe the remedies. Responsibility returned to the people who lived through the catastrophe which life, under French domination, had so long represented.

We must remember, as we judge the present in the independent Maghrib, that though we have some little perspective in the cases of Morocco and Tunisia, where independence enters its ninth year, in Algeria, the second phase of the revolution has scarcely begun. Yet, as time unfolds and future turns into past, the mixture of Islam plus Europeanization plus independence will almost surely offer something unique in the world.

TUNISIA

The Tunisian Adjustment

Tunisia, the smallest, least populated, and poorest in natural resources of the former French holdings in the Maghrib, made the jump to independence with the least difficulty. It is possible that France did not care quite as much about losing Tunisia as she would about Morocco, and, of course, she was determined *not* to give up Algeria. Tunisia's difficulties were less than her sister states in the realm of political institutions, economic development, and in the basic cultural zone where the struggle to adjust the Islamic base of society to the aberration of the colonial past, and to the future needs of the new state, became a consuming passion. The reasons for this are not complicated compared to Morocco and Algeria. Tunisia possessed a mature nationalist organization, the Neo-Destour party, which, on independence day, held the nation's confidence in hand. Its case had been carefully explained, not only to the city worker, but to the peasantry. Its excellent leaders, especially Bourguiba, commanded general respect, and these men developed a realistic program which took into account the fact that Carthage was not built, nor could it be rebuilt, in a day.

Elections to the Constituent Assembly gave the party 97 per cent of the vote. This meant that if the party remained united and continued to enjoy national support, Tunisia was at least on the road toward responsible, efficient government, a prerequisite for an attack upon the gigantic economic and social problems.

Bourguiba served as head of state when the Beylical system was painlessly discarded (July 1957); and, then, under the constitution, he was elected president. The constitution vested impressive powers in the executive who was elected by universal male suffrage for a term of five years and could be reelected twice. Bourguiba's authority resembles that of the American president. Among other things, he can issue executive orders when the assembly is in recess. He holds, as does the president of France's Fifth Republic, broad emergency powers. The legislature, while not by any means a rubber stamp, since it had to approve the budget and held a veto if it could muster a two-thirds majority, in practice yielded to the popular president.

Local government functioned through the cooperation of a governor and an elected council. In a small state divided into thirteen provincial units, the relationship between local and central authorities was intimate, but governors nevertheless made important decisions. Since independence the most impressive change related to personal status.

When the new code became the law in 1957, Tunisia, the first Arab state to do so, abolished polygamy and gave women equality before the law. No longer could the male simply denounce his spouse three times and disappear into the desert. Women and children obtained a legal protection previously unknown in the Arabic world. The improvement of women's status brought half the population, previously passive, into direct national participation, and strengthened the Neo-Destour party immeasurably. The law became secular and equal for every citizen regardless of sex or religion, and this, by Western standards a basic human right, represented a great Tunisian advancement.

No Berber separatism plagued the Neo-Destour, whose top leaders have been likened to members of the same intimate club. These men came out of strong French schools or from Sadiqi College. Apart from the sharp division with Ben Youssef and his followers, Bourguiba and his followers faced no powerful rivals. Ben Youssef himself was the victim of a political assassination in 1961, and the next year an assassination attempt was made on Bourguiba, possibly by *Youssefistes*. Through all this, Bourguiban stability was remarkable. There have been public differences, as for example with Masmoudi on religious and foreign policy questions or with Ben Salah on economic issues, but the presidential heart has usually been big; and the spirit of the opposition large enough to remain in the fold. After the ill-fated Bizerte operation in 1961, Bourguiba's stock most surely fell in the Maghrib and throughout Africa. At home, however, apart from the disappointment of young party militants, his popularity held strong. The unsuccessful plot on his life probably helped restore his position. There is no dearth of able Tunisian men, as the presence of Mongi Slim (who served in many posts, including that of President of the United Nations) and Bahi Ladgham (possibly Bourguiba's successor) will testify. Yet we know too little about the generation of younger men, in their thirties and forties, such as Taieb Mehiri, the capable minister of the interior, to judge the drift of the future.

Whether Neo-Destour will continue to hold the people, to inspire their unity, and obtain freely given sacrifice is a moot question. Thus far, the party has provided the armature on which the administration built its program. It will remain to be seen if the party ossifies, becomes staid, loses its creativity and driving force, becomes a part of the establishment. Much will depend upon the incoming new blood. The young men must not only be intelligent, but they must be aware of new goals.

Young militant members of the Neo-Destour who demanded greater civil rights at home (Arab socialism) and who favored Nasser-neutralism abroad rather than orientation toward the West, clearly understood that their efficacy was limited. Bourguiba could drive them out of the party through his control of the Political Bureau, and through the High Court, which operated in Star Chamber fashion, and he could imprison them. The three mass trials of the *Youssefistes* and the resulting executions (1956-1959) kept would-be critics in bounds. Ideas and suggestions from the next generation of Neo-Destour's leaders were welcomed, but opposition, pressed to the point of coup d'état, becomes treason.

After nine years of independence it is almost impossible to find men in the upper or middle party brackets who do not fill a responsible place in the administration. They are literally married to the movement and spend practically all their waking hours in government or party work.

Trade Balances

All the Maghribi countries are economically underdeveloped according to the usually accepted measuring sticks. Per capita income at independence in Tunisia was $130 per year, lower than Morocco at $190 and Algeria, measured in 1958 at $200. For Muslims alone these figures would be considerably lower because European incomes are included in the average. Tunisia, unfortunately, possesses almost no exploitable sources of energy, certainly, to date, no discovered oil, and much of the soil is barren or marginal.

In each country there are two widely separated economies—a modern European commercial-agricultural type, which invests in industries and land, and a primitive indigenous kind which employs traditional methods and scarcely ever intersects with the developed economy. In independent Morocco and Tunisia no startling agrarian changes have yet taken place. The first eighteen months of Algerian independence, however, witnessed the beginnings of an agrarian reform effort, which arose out of necessity. Another common denominator of the economy of each country is its link with France. Normally, 55 per cent of Tunisia's import-export trade was with France. In Morocco, the figures are slightly lower, while in Algeria's case, before independence, 80 per cent of incoming and outgoing goods came from or went to France. Even after the hectic period of adjustment to independence passes, this trade should continue strong because of joint interest in the Sahara, and because French aid to Algeria far outdistances any other outside contribution.

At the outset of independence, Tunisia and Morocco remained in the franc zone. More recently they freed themselves from the franc, concluded bilateral agreements outside the zone, and, in Tunisia's case, ended the customs union with France. Despite this show of economic independence, both countries still maintain close credit ties with the Bank of France. The Evian accords placed Algeria inside the zone and, thus far, the independent state's interest surely lies in that direction. Both Tunisia and Morocco have somewhat reduced their deficient trade balances, but until productivity can be raised, mileage along this road is severely limited. All underdeveloped countries find it extremely difficult to break existing trade patterns with the more industrialized states, particularly with the former colonial mother countries; but as Charles Gallagher succinctly notes, "an elastic membership in a monetary and trading area like the franc zone can be made to cover almost any contingency." [1]

For many decades, all of North Africa suffered from unemployment and underemployment. The gap between available work and population grew wider and wider as the twentieth century passed its half-way point. During the late colonial period, this same situation prevailed, but it was screened by the presence of Europeans. Since independence, it remains the number one socio-economic issue. How can unemployment be reduced, or better, eliminated? The theoretical answer is simple enough, by bringing more land under cultivation, using modern techniques, and possibly by redistribution and planned rational planting. At the same time, industries must be built to provide work for the ever-increasing urban population and to mechanize ag-

[1] Charles F. Gallagher, *The United States and North Africa, Morocco, Algeria, and Tunisia* (Cambridge, Mass.: Harvard, 1963), p. 155.

riculture. To transform the theory into a program requires trained scientific, technological, and administrative cadres, and capital. This last must be gotten in the world money markets or taken out of the people's labor. In general, these farmers and workers achieve no more than a marginal subsistence: they would face starvation if part of their existing income were deducted. So these countries must have outside aid in capital and in facilities to train the necessary cadres, which are inadequate, though not hopelessly scarce (as is in the case of the Congo).

Are the likely sources of this support in Cairo, Moscow, Peiping, or Havana? Educational exchange and some technicians may come from these underdeveloped countries, and reams of ideological support, but they themselves face grave economic problems, particularly of the Algerian type. In the foreseeable future, the West is the obvious candidate for help. But French private capital, and much of that in the other money markets, is frightened; almost a billion dollars in French capital left Algeria in 1962. Even so, state aid from the West is the largest source. And this becomes a difficult political question too, both inside the North African states and in the West where the individual taxpayers have some, albeit remote, control over spending. Thus far, the lion's share of state aid comes from France, the state which still does the most business in North Africa. In the case of Algeria, French aid appears to be leveling off at roughly the same amount as the Algerian deficit in trade balance before 1954, about $200,00,000 per year.

Land reform becomes, then, an imperative in these and all underdeveloped countries. But it must be accompanied by a related concern for industrial expansion. In Tunisia's case, a far-reaching program, beginning in 1956, led to state acquisition of the *habous* lands totalling approximately one quarter of the cultivated surface. At the same time, 4,000,000 acres of tribal lands were shifted to individual holders. Two years later plans were laid to purchase property held by Europeans, but a slender beginning was cut short by the Bizerte crisis during which some 130,000 acres belonging to Europeans were expropriated. Settlement of this claim was agreed upon before France finally withdrew from Bizerte, late in 1963.

Bourguiba's "New Deal" Plan

Beginning in 1959, Bourguiba introduced a large public works program, reminiscent of the New Deal in the United States, which aimed to rehabilitate the unemployed by providing work on various projects. At the same time, these projects, when completed, would increase national productivity and pay the labor costs. They were financed by the state at subsistence level pay. According to reliable witnesses, this program achieved substantial success. In important measure, the Neo-Destour, by rallying the national will and imposing discipline, contributed to this result. Such control was absolutely indispensable to convince the urban unemployed to return to their villages for work. Another "plus factor" related to the nice balance between central and local government which allowed goals to be selected in the villages or districts yet planned and supported in Tunis. Finally, the program enabled a large number of Tunisians to learn new techniques, in the process of staying alive and building something for their state.

Tunisia, though a one party state, has not become oppressive the way many fascist and communist one-party states have. The outsider, accustomed to an intended inefficiency of law enforcement in small matters in Europe or the United States, may sometimes find Tunisian officials heavy-handed and unduly serious in the discharge of their duties. Small functionaries in the new states take themselves seriously because respect for the new order becomes an important matter. Without it there could be the return to organized anarchy which some Anglo-Saxons found so characteristic in the French Third and Fourth Republics. These new states took a page from the recent French political notebook and tried to avoid the fairly sterile game of multiparty politics in an all-powerful assembly which so consistently shot down ministers and led to *immobilisme*. Since the ordinary Tunisian was fairly docile and amenable to compromise, he needed an active paternalism to move him. This may well change as the nation gains political maturity and if visible economic progress can be made.

Looking ahead to independent Tunisia's condition a decade hence, we see a clear set of targets set up by the National Planning Council. No man can say, with any certainty, whether these goals for 1971 will be attained. What is abundantly clear, however, is that Tunisia has "chosen the way of discipline because it is the way of reason," in the words of Bourguiba. It is equally apparent, that after seven years of independence, the struggle to develop has barely begun. This fact must certainly encourage the opposition of young malcontents in the party system.

During the period 1950-1959, the annual average rate of increase of resources as a whole amounted to 1.6 per cent. Targets for the ten year plan (1962-1971) rest upon an annual 6 per cent increase in the gross domestic product. But this basic objective highlights the gigantic effort expected of the people. Considering Tunisia's leadership, party solidarity, and the enormous potential of a population in which nearly 40 per cent is under age fourteen, there are some hopeful indications, barring unexpected disaster, that these goals can be approached.[2]

MOROCCO

Post-Independence Politics in Morocco

Politics in independent Morocco did not run so smoothly. Morocco was larger, its people more activist in nature, more diversified, and the king was deeply engaged, along with Istiqlal, in the nationalist cause, whereas the Bey was outside the nationalist movement in Tunisia. Morocco, like Algeria, possessed a large and restless Berber population which had to be somehow accommodated in political institutions. It might be good form and even good colonial policy, at least at given stages, for the French to divide the Berbers from the Arabs, but the Moroccan king in 1956 could never so view his subjects.

Morocco's first task was to restore order, a difficult one given the underground ramifications of various terrorist groups who fought the French in the cities, plus the Liberation Army's free operation in the countryside. Slowly the police got the upper hand in the cities after some fairly large battles. "Good" urban resistance was incorporated directly into the police force. In the countryside, the Liberation Army threatened to remain a separate striking force. Some units joined the

[2] See *Tunisian Development*, 62-71, published by the Secretariat of State for Cultural Affairs and Information (Tunis, 1962), for 200 pages of important statistical information and projections.

royal army but, in the south, Allal al-Fassi, the prominent Istiqlal leader, asserted claims to the French and Spanish Sahara and hoped to use the Liberation Army to bolster the Algerian National Liberation Front's struggle against the French. In November 1957, a strike against Spanish Ifni failed. At the same time some Liberation Army leaders organized the Popular Movement, a new political party devoted to Islamic socialism.

During the first four years of independence, political conditions defied stabilization. No satisfactory working relationship between Mohammed V and the Istiqlal party emerged and, by 1960, the king abandoned his above-politics position and led the government himself. Meanwhile Istiqlal split up. In the first cabinet, that of Si Bekkai, who was Mohammed's man, Istiqlal demanded more posts. Given all the cabinet places in the second Si Bekkai cabinet, Istiqlal complained that the king by-passed the cabinet through the crown council.

By this time, Istiqlal leaders, such as Mehdi Ben Barka, Abdallah Ibrahim, and Abderrahim Bouabid, believed that the older party fathers were unresponsive to the needs of the masses. An open controversy between the two groups was fought through the press, which tolerated considerable freedom of expression.

Balafrej formed a government based upon the older, more conservative Istiqlal elements, in May 1958. But this approach failed in December, largely because chronic economic problems in the cities, and the Rif, where violence broke out, gave Ben Barka's wing a constant target. Mohammed V decided to allow these reformists or progressives some responsibility, so he appointed a caretaker cabinet, under Ibrahim, which was expected to prepare elections. Actually, this government served more than a year but did not relieve the economic crisis. Nor did it heal the Istiqlal schism or bring political peace. Instead, by mid-1959 the Istiqlal progressives formed a new party, the National Union of Popular Forces (UNFP), which attracted leaders of the Moroccan Trade Union (UMT) and various other restless, frustrated groups. The conservative Istiqlal elements countered by founding a rival trade union in the hope of appealing to the working class.

Unlike the Tunisians who took their politics calmly and who never smashed the basic unity of the Neo-Destour, the Moroccans were willing to secede from Istiqlal and to fight in the streets for their political views. The Ibrahim government lacked any force to prevent these clashes and the king refused to commit troops in a domestic brawl. The situation then drifted toward chaos and in so doing demonstrated the inability of Moroccan parties to deal constructively with pressing issues. Mohammed V then terminated the Ibrahim government and formed a national coalition under himself, with Crown Prince Moulay Hassan as vice premier. All the parties save the UNFP supported this new approach.

The decision threw the enormous prestige of the monarchy into the midst of practical day-to-day politics, and it stabilized the situation. In general, the crown's greatest zone of support lay among the conservative urban dwellers and all sectors of rural Morocco. But so great was respect for Mohammed V in both the political and religious realms that even the industrial masses who leaned toward the UNFP curbed their tongues and their demonstrators. The first five years of independence clearly proved Morocco's need for a strong leader, and Mohammed V discharged his vast power with benevolence and wisdom. His untimely death in February 1961, after minor surgery, brought on unprecedented mourning among his people. Young Hassan II then became Sultan. Well-educated and experienced as he was, he could not hope to replace in the hearts of the Moroccan people, a father who had been a rare political phenomenon—a revolutionary king.

The Rule of Hassan II

A constitution, tailored to please the royal will, received the overwhelming acceptance of the nation, expressed in a referendum held in 1962. In the ratio of thirty-seven to one, the people approved the idea that Morocco was a "constitutional, social, democratic" monarchy whose religion was Islam and language Arabic. Underlining its affinity with the Maghribi neighbors and envisioning a future united Africa, the constitution pointedly omitted the concept of Pan-Arabism. The powers of the king remained exceedingly impressive. He could dissolve parliament once a year and he named the ministers who, incidentally, could be voted out by parliament. The king kept the right to by-pass the legislature and to submit measures by referendum to the people. An assembly elected by universal suffrage and a council elected by notables, was expected to help govern, but its power was strictly secondary to the crown.

Since 1963, Morocco's political evolution structurally resembled the Fifth Republic in striking fashion. Early in that year, a new party, the equivalent of de Gaulle's UNR, the Front for the Defense of Constitutional Institutions (FDIC), took form as a Crown party. It obtained the support of the Popular Movement, in turn based upon a rural and Berber following. The old line Istiqlal, built upon the urban middle-class and religious leaders, refused to play the rôle of the militant opposition, but the UNFP accepted that responsibility.

One of the lustiest attacks against Hassan II and the leader of the FDIC, Ahmed Guedira, minister of interior and agriculture, was delivered in April 1963, by Al-Fassi, who took the king to task for not pressing Morocco's claim to Mauretania, a desert area to the south which became independent, with Franco-Tunisian support, in 1960. Moroccan nationalists always considered Mauretania part of Morocco, and when it appeared that Hassan II and the FDIC were dropping all claims, Al-Fassi spoke out directly and critically. Guedira quickly noted that though Morocco's claim to Mauretania was a solid one, it had complicated Morocco's relationship with the African states which supported Mauretanian independence.

In the May 1963, parliamentary elections the FDIC failed to obtain the hoped-for majority and suffered a psychological defeat. Of the 144 seats, it won 69, and seven of its nine ministers who presented themselves as candidates lost. Istiqlal obtained 41 seats, while the left-wing UNFP received 28, and the independents 6. Though this result did not alter the basis of power which rested in Hassan's hands, it was important since the Chamber of Representatives exercised budgetary powers and was a sounding board for the king's program. By July, some 130 leaders of the National Union of Popular Forces (UNFP) were arrested, accused of plotting against "the security of the state . . . and aiming to take power with the overthrow of the regime by violent measures."

Both the Istiqlal and UNFP claimed Hassan II was setting aside, even arresting or placing under strict surveillance, many former nationalist leaders. Al-Fassi remained untouched but he estimated that 4,000 members of Istiqlal had been interrogated and hundreds detained. Student and labor union leaders were among those held. Ben Barka fled into voluntary exile in Geneva; former premier Ibrahim was placed under surveillance along with Bouabid. Surrounding Hassan II were Guedira, director of palace staff, minister of agriculture, and leader of the royalist front FDIC; Mohamed Oufkir, director of national security, and Colonel Driss Ben Amar, governor of Casablanca, men who earlier stood close to the French administration and who had been hostile to nationalist leaders. The minister of interior, Ahmed Hamiani willingly recognized Ben Arafa as Sultan at the time of Mohammed V's dethronement (1953).

This development appeared to be the logical outcome of direct intervention by the crown into politics, an action which appeared necessary in 1960 when Mohammed V formed a coalition ministry. By late 1963, however, the coalition represented a less effective position. It had become narrower and the Istiqlal and UNFP, by combining, could balance the FDIC royalist front. Once again Moroccan political evolution resembled that of the Fifth Republic and, with power in the royal hands, party strength was somewhat irrelevant.

A new cabinet, considered moderate and pro Western took shape in November, 1963. Ahmed Bahnini, a former minister of justice who had served as president of the supreme court, became premier, an indication that Hassan II moved toward a position above day-to-day politics. Guedira replaced Balafrej as foreign minister and the latter became personal representative of the king with the rank of minister. No member of Istiqlal or the UNFP sat in the new cabinet. The pressure against the Istiqlal progressives and the UNFP, plus the political complexion of the cabinet, indicated that Hassan II refused a forced march toward socialism at home or toward a close relationship with Egypt and Pan-Arabism.

The Moroccan Economy

Independent Morocco launched no revolutionary plans to transform the economy. Moderation and deliberation have characterized both agrarian and industrial planning. As elsewhere in North Africa, one of the serious facts of life in the underdeveloped state is that population increases at 2-3 per cent per year. This is more rapid than the growth in cereal production and pasturage and leads straight toward starvation. Earlier French efforts to diversify agricultural production by the introduction of rice, expansion of cotton acreage, irrigation, and vine cultivation brought some relief. But they failed to alter the basic population-food productivity ratio, largely because European-owned lands emphasized production of export commodities which obviously did not feed the growing Moroccan population. In 1957 a cooperative farming undertaking tried to increase output. It provided farmers with seeds and fertilizer and urged them to subscribe to a state tractor service. The farmer paid the state $15 per hectare for the service. Yield was increased on some 300,000 hectares, but the plan ran into peasant reluctance to change from traditional techniques and did not flourish.

Through a plan known as *Promotion Nationale*, Hassan II, in 1961, began a serious attack upon rural poverty and illiteracy. Local authorities gathered together the under-employed and set them to work on small-scale irrigation projects, reforestation, land drainage, and canal building. Paid forty cents per day plus the same amount in wheat, flour, or rice, these workers planted 17,000,000 trees, dug 600 miles of canals, and repaired 1800 miles of road in the first year. In that same year an estimated 7,000,000 additional working days had been provided.

Hassan II created Communal Centers to manage local affairs. The heretofore passive rural inhabitant was transformed into a participating citizen. He reacted by taking pride in building more than the estimated quota of classrooms and actively worked in public programs in his home area. Thus, the local inhabitant joined his loyalty to home or village with the broader interests and needs of the state.

European owners in Morocco were not hit by expropriation or sequestration but they were urged to make decisions which would conform to the national need. In 1962 a cadastral survey (whose ultimate object was to unify land fragments so common in Islamic countries), designed to rationalize cultivation and thereby increase yield, moved forward.

At the outset of independence, the flight of European capital and the closing down of enterprises retarded the new state's advancement. Shortage of capital continually plagues development, and statutes prepared by the Bureau of Studies and Industrial Participation (BEPI) tried to attract capital by promising customs privileges, rights to transfer dividends, and various preferential arrangements. Outside investors were told they had the word of the state that nationalization would not take place. No spectacular results occurred, but Morocco advanced its phosphate and chemical industry.

The nationalization of French property in independent Algeria, under Ben Bella, prompted Istiqlal and the National Union of Popular Forces in Morocco to demand "authentic reform." But thus far, Hassan II and Guedira refuse to yield and, instead, sought support from the capital markets of the West. In April 1963, when Hassan II returned from Washington, he faced demands from labor for wage increases in order to protect the wage earners from an increased living cost of 9.7 per cent since January 1962, according to official statistics. Token strikes took place in the mines and elsewhere.

Guedira stated publicly that in his opinion, the heart of Morocco's problem of productivity stemmed from traditional Muslim attitudes. Modern concepts of work, saving, and investment he found to be quite foreign to the Moroccan intellectual and spiritual heritage. That changes in outlook will take place in the future seems extremely likely, particularly when one bears in mind that increasingly large numbers of North Africans are studying abroad, not solely in France, but throughout the world. The dynamic new generation in the Maghrib is materialistic in the sense that it wants better jobs, food, housing, clothes, books, records, etc. What it requires is capital, a trained labor force, the necessary raw materials, and the techniques of bringing all these together to make a product for a market. In Morocco, the capitalist road seems far more open than in newly-independent Algeria. Throughout the Maghrib, however, enterprise or entrepreneurship will have to serve the interests of the nation and will be frowned upon where it too closely resembles older nineteenth century European colonial patterns.

ALGERIA

Independence and Division in Algeria

During the Algerian revolution, the outside world learned astonishingly little of the factions which played upon one another within the Algerian leadership. Messali Hadj and his followers were known to be trouble-makers in France and Algeria, and there were some bloody battles fought in both places, between the FLN and Messalists. Informed observers, like Serge and Merry Bromberger, likewise guessed that rivalry, if not jealousy, would develop between the "internals," those who fought inside Algeria with short odds against the French, and the "externals" who sat first in Cairo, later in Tunis. And rivalry could be expected in the case of the ALN, Algerian Liberation Army, between the soldiers who deployed outside the Challe-Morice lines, who sometimes harassed or broke through the barriers with men and equipment, and the Freedom Fighters who fought practically every day in the *wilayas* in Algeria. It was probably also true that the internals often fell under Kabyle leaders who were Berber in background and spirit, while the externals, particularly the Cairo group, were Arabs. Differing ends were esteemed by the old guard classless leaders of the OS and the johnny-come-lately (to the FLN) bourgeois respectables like Ferhat Abbas and Ahmed Francis of the UDMA (*Union Démocratique du Manifeste Algérien*). Finally, four major figures languished in French custody after 1956. These four, Ben Bella, Aït Ahmed, Khider, and Boudiaf were "originals"; they pondered the Algerian revolution and their place in it during the nearly six years' detention, and, when they were released, they had much to say and much time to make up.

The great schism came at the CNRA (National Council of the Algerian Revolution) meeting held in Tripoli in May 1962, after the Evian accords and before independence. There, the four kidnapped ministers, recently released, resumed an active part in the revolution. Treaty-making is a heavy responsibility and Ben Bella had already served notice on the Provisional Government of the Algerian Republic (GPRA) that it had "confiscated the revolution." At the CNRA meeting no agreement was reached on the composition of the vital Political Committee which would prepare the list of FLN (National Liberation Front) candidates for election to the future assembly. Here was where ultimate power would rest, since only one party would present candidates. Ben Bella proposed the four "kidnapped" ministers plus Said Mohammedi, who once served as Krim's eastern zone commander (and who became "notoriously anti-Krim"), for the Political Bureau. No satisfactory majority supported this move, nor could the proposal to name Ben Bella, Ben Khedda, who was premier of the GPRA at the time, Krim, Boudiaf, and Abbas succeed.

At that impasse, Krim, Ben Khedda, and the majority of the GPRA left the meeting as if to say they would stand upon their office and their accomplishments and continue to run things. This action brought the quick denunciation of Ben Bella, Khider, Rabah Bitat, various ALN leaders, and Abbas. In June, both factions tried to strengthen themselves inside Algeria. The GPRA accused the ALN general staff of counterrevolution and dismissed it, on paper. One member, Major Slimane, was temporarily arrested. Boumedienne, the chief of staff who supported Ben Bella, survived, and naturally the outspoken Slimane. Ben Bella himself fled to Tripoli to escape the GPRA. The ALN refused to accept the GPRA as more than an agent of the National Council of the Algerian Revolution, as indeed it was, and stood firm.

Ben Bella Comes to Power

This was the scene of division within the Algerian high command on independence day, and it became worse before it got better. After nearly eight years of unity during a very hard war, here they were, the staunch leaders, blasted apart by a little success. This spectacle must have been a bitter thing to watch from inside Algeria; and on the outside, world opinion took cognizance once more of the old fact that it is sometimes easier to be a hero than a peace-maker. One element in the situation, however, fortunately died out. This was the Secret Army of European die-hards and their hired killers, the terrorist force of the colons, whose leaders scattered across all the borders as independence approached.

Elections were supposed to take place three weeks after independence, roughly July 25, 1962. But until electoral lists could be prepared, they were held in abeyance. Those crucial lists would powerfully influence the future direction of Algeria and whoever controlled them would control the regime. A political committee would draw the lists, but who would compose the committee? The power struggle lay between Ben Bella, who returned to Marna, in west Algeria, his birthplace and stronghold, and the GPRA remnants who had deserted the last CNRA meeting. Particularly active in opposition to Ben Bella, were Krim and Boudiaf. *Wilaya* leaders sought unsuccessfully to mediate. From Oran, Ben Bella announced a political committee. Krim and Boudiaf turned thumbs down on this maneuver and began to organize resistance in *wilaya* III, the Kabylia, in order to counterbalance opposing forces in the west and the Constantine. Momentarily, an accord was reached between Ben Bella and the Kabyle captains, and he came to Algiers.

A dispute over the size of the ALN, with Ben Bella demanding reduction of the force, and *wilaya* IV (Algiers region), whose commanders opposed him, led to his early return to Oran. He who held the military force would probably name the Political Committee. Ben Bella's military support lay with those units of the ALN which operated outside the Challe-Morice lines and with Boumedienne, their chief of staff. The Kabyles obviously did not want their forces reduced until the Political Committee was named.

This time, Ben Bella ordered troops in the west to march upon Algiers. Meanwhile *wilaya* IV dug in to resist. Along this march enough fighting took place, at points like Aumale, to result in perhaps several hundred dead. Boumedienne's forces had recently received heavier equipment from outside Algeria, and this helped decide the outcome. As the two factions fired upon one another, the people were sickened. Civilians moved in protest demonstration, even lying down in the road between the two forces, and in the cities the shout *"Assez,"* Enough, was heard in French and Arabic. Within four days the National Popular Army (ANP), the new name of the ALN, entered Algiers.

Ben Bella formed the Political Committee; an amended list of candidates eliminated some thirty names, including Ben Khedda, and other opponents of Ben Bella, and became the official and sole electoral list. Many outside observers who had built up faith in the GPRA faction which had so well conducted the closing years of the war, were disappointed to see this narrowing of the lists, this strengthening of a one-party system. It seemed only too obvious that Algeria needed to use all its talent at this crucial time, not just a fraction of it. The election, a mere formality, ratified Ben Bella's list, and on September

29 the Assembly met under the presidency of Ferhat Abbas to confirm the government of Ben Bella.

Scarcely a week later, Algeria entered the United Nations. A ten-person delegation headed by the premier, including Khemisti, the foreign minister, Tewfik Al-Madani, the Islamic affairs minister, Yazid, the sole official survivor of the GPRA named to the Assembly, Major Slimane of the ALN, Chanderli, New York Algerian Office chief, Mme Nemmiche, the widow of *wilaya* commander Loufti, and Father Berenguer, a French priest who joined the FLN, came to New York. Ben Bella's acceptance speech in the United Nations gave notice that Algeria would be non-aligned, neutral, but not passive in the affairs of the nations. His country, he said, would stand for pacific regulation of international problems. The People's Republic of China, he thought, must join the United Nations. Ben Bella's address ended on the note "Peace, Men, Good Will," but he warned that peace would continue to elude mankind until the disparity between the living standards of the "Third World" and the Western world had been equalized.

From New York he visited Washington, then Cuba, a state whose relationship to America reminded him of Algeria's relationship to France, and which had cared for a number of ALN wounded during the rebellion. He was eager to see what was happening inside the experimental socialist regime of Fidel Castro. They faced many similar problems.

Then he returned home to the political and economic wars of a new country. Ben Bella's political axe soon fell upon the Algerian Communist party, which he dissolved.

Algeria began its political life with one party, the FLN, which was broad enough, its spokesmen argued, to accommodate all views. Possibly, too, the FLN leadership felt that an active Algerian Communist party would embarrass the new state's neutral stance in international politics. One can conjecture that the decisions to ban the party arose out of unsatisfactory experience with the local communists during the revolution, or just possibly the leaders understood that such a ban would strike a satisfactory note in the money markets of the West without entirely alienating aid from the East. With the UGTA, the Algerian trade union, which hoped to maintain a posture outside politics, Ben Bella was more gentle; but in essence he brought it under FLN control.

Politics and Constitution-Making

In the Algerian Assembly, Aït Ahmed, the Kabyle leader and one of the fathers of the FLN, spoke up frequently against Ben Bella and the government's program. Boudiaf, another "original," refused to take his seat in the assembly, as a protest against the means used to prepare the lists. A clandestine Party of the Socialist Revolution for a brief period probed Algeria's political wounds from the ultra-Marxist viewpoint. Ben Bella seemingly stood fast against this opposition. In April 1963, Khider resigned as secretary general of the political bureau and Ben Bella assumed this title. Though Khider, who was one of the founding fathers of the FLN, supported Ben Bella at the outset of independence, he announced that "fundamental differences" forced his resignation. Possibly Ben Bella's pragmatic approach could not be squared with Khider's more ideological posture on Algerian socialism and Arab unity. Rumor also had it that Khider wished an FLN party congress to draft a constitution, while the premier viewed this as the work of the government and the Assembly committee, together with party leaders.

The next political casualty was Ferhat Abbas who resigned as President of the Assembly in August 1963. Earlier he had complained of the rapid plunge toward socialism and one-man rule. It was quite clear that neither the revolution's direction in the first year of independence nor the forthcoming constitution pleased the old bourgeois leader of the UDMA. Two months earlier Boudiaf and three other opponents of Ben Bella's march upon Algiers had been arrested and placed in "comfortable detainment" in the Sahara area. Boudiaf was released five months later. Upon the occasion of Boudiaf's arrest, a lively exchange took place between Aït Ahmed and Ben Bella in the Assembly.

Aït Ahmed complained of the deterioration of the country, of police state measures, and questioned the rhythm of the socialist march. His motion for a full scale debate lost by a heavy majority but thirty deputies abstained. Ben Bella defended the arrests as necessary to the security of the state. He labeled the arrested persons as "political adventurers" and claimed no other country in Africa allowed its citizens "to speak so freely, to criticize, and even lead criminal political activity." Again, on July 2, 1963, in a statement published outside the Assembly, Aït Ahmed returned to the attack upon Ben Bella as a "man who is all powerful, blind, and obsessed." He called for a "peaceful debate" on Algerian socialism, the regime, and the National Liberation Front party. He called for a government of national unity.

One reason political fever ran high in the late summer of 1963 was that the new constitution was taking shape. Prepared by the Constitutional Committee of the Assembly and the FLN high command, it passed the Assembly on August 28 by a vote of 139 to 23 with 8 abstentions. In the preceding free debate, the opposition fixed upon the provisions which granted the FLN, as the sole political party, the power to name the president and Assembly. What bothered these critics was the lack of definition in party structure; in short they questioned its base as too narrow and not representative of the whole nation. A referendum held on September 8 resulted in the approval of 98 per cent of the voters but Aït Ahmed ordered his followers in the Kabylia mountains to abstain and many did. Even so, of 6,391,818 eligible voters, 5,283,994 voted, according to the official result. The turnout, by western standards, was heavy.[3]

Two days later, 3,500 FLN party delegates, meeting in the Majestic Cinema in Algiers, named Ben Bella as the party's official presidential candidate. Colonel Houari Boumedienne, vice premier and defense minister, pledged the army's support to Ben Bella and deprecated "separatists" who would split the army and the FLN. The following Sunday, another referendum overwhelmingly endorsed the nomination by a vote of 5,548,704 to 18,355 with some 749,742 registered voters abstaining. Elections to the Assembly were postponed for one year, at which time, according to the new constitution, the Assembly would be assured a life of five years.[4]

To his critics in the Kabylia, Aït Ahmed, and Krim who resigned his seat in the Assembly and went to Switzerland, Ben Bella had this suggestion. "I ask them to come to us so that we can all work together for the national good. I will never be anything else but a disinterested

[3] *El Moudjahid*, Algiers, September 14, 1963.
[4] *Le Monde*, September 17, 1963.

militant. There is a place for criticism, a place to seek change, but it is in the Front, not in the foreign press." [5] He again denied all interest in the cult of personality and claimed the Algerian people would never accept dictatorship. He noted, too, in commenting on the charge of repression, that there had not been a single execution since independence. This last statement applied, no doubt, to legal executions. It was no secret that a large number of *harki*, Algerians who served in the French army, were lynched after independence.

Algeria's constitution declared the state to be an integral part of the Maghrib, the Arab world, and of Africa. "Islam is the religion of the State. The Republic guarantees the respect of opinions and beliefs and the free exercise of all religions." Arabic became the official language but French was acceptable, pending Arabization. Torture was outlawed. Article 12 read: "All the citizens of both sexes have the same rights and duties," but these rights for women were not implemented in law and custom. (The day Aït Ahmed opened his attack on Ben Bella in the Assembly, that body was discussing a proposal to outlaw marriage for girls under sixteen.)

Complete power rested in a sole party, the FLN, which in turn controlled "the action of the National Assembly and the Government." Article 24 allowed the FLN to define the policy of the nation and inspire the action of the state. The executive through which this power flowed was the president of the republic, elected by universal suffrage for five years after nomination by the party. Candidates for this office had to be Muslims and at least thirty-five years old. The president held practically unlimited powers, though many of these involved consultation with, and support of the National Assembly. He was obliged to select at least two-thirds of the ministers from the deputies, and he could be voted out of office by a censure passed by an absolute majority of the Assembly acting upon a petition signed by one-third of the deputies. Such a vote automatically dissolved the National Assembly. The president of the Assembly would fill in as president of the republic in the event of incapacity, resignation, or censure of the president of the republic, and would prepare new election within two months.[6]

[5] *The New York Times*, September 11, 1963.
[6] Text of constitution in *El Moudjahid*, September 7, 1963.

In selecting ministries Ben Bella invariably relied upon men of proved personal loyalty. Khemisti, his first foreign minister, thirty-three years old, had been his neighbor in Marna. Ben Bella watched him grow up and brought him to Cairo with him before 1954. When Khemisti was assassinated in April 1963, the premier took over the ministry; in September, when he named a new government, Abdelaziz Bouteflika, a long-standing cohort and former minister of youth, received the post. Ali Mahsas, who replaced the ailing Omar Ouzegane as minister of agriculture, had been in prison in Blida with Ben Bella in 1952. Later he handled various important missions and is credited with warning Ben Bella of a Red Hand plot to kill him in Tripoli in 1955. Hadj Smaïn, the new minister of justice, served in the Battle of Algiers in 1956 and, after 1962, was Ben Bella's personal secretary and *directeur de cabinet*. So great were the obstacles to political peace and economic development that talent plus loyalty seemed absolute prerequisites for high office in the first years of Ben Bella's leadership. After all the years of clandestine planning and active rebellion, it was scarcely surprising that revolutionary chiefs transformed to presidents valued devotion.

The influence of the ALN also was apparent in the new cabinet, especially that branch of the army which served closely with Boumedienne outside the *wilayas*. Boumedienne himself continued, as first vice-president of the council and defense minister, while Ahmed Kaid (Major Slimane) became minister of tourism and Cherif Belkacem (Major Djemmal) was appointed minister of orientation. Rabah Bitat, old member of the OS (*organisation spéciale*) which planned the 1954 uprising, was reappointed third vice-president of the council but he declined the office, in front of television cameras, on the grounds that his post was simply honorary. He had supported Khider in the spring struggle for control of the FLN and lost.[7]

In October 1963, the new regime faced a double challenge. Aït Ahmed and other Kabylia leaders announced they would return to the mountains in order to resist the dictatorship of Ben Bella. Shortly after, skirmishing between Algerian and Moroccan troops broke out on the ill-defined southwestern Algerian frontier. After approximately two weeks of sporadic fighting between relatively small numbers of

[7] *Le Monde*, September 19, 1963, for the list of the cabinet.

troops, Algeria and Morocco agreed to submit the dispute to the new Organization of African Unity (OAU) for study. Representatives from seven African states, Ethiopia, Mali, Senegal, Ivory Coast, Republic of Sudan, Tanganyika, and Nigeria, assumed this task for OAU. Algeria's position was that borders inherited from colonial powers could not be questioned. Morocco based its claim to the western Sahara on historical maps and unfinished negotiations between Morocco and France at the time of Algerian independence.

The frontier war pulled the rug from under the Kabylia resistance movement. National unity took precedence over what *Le Monde* called the "last hope for all the Algerian bourgeoisie directly attacked by Ben Bella." When Mohand Ou El Hadj, the Kabyle military leader, made his peace with Ben Bella, Aït Ahmed was isolated. The latter still insisted, however, that the single party FLN should be broadened to include all tendencies which had won the war of independence. He seemed also to be objecting to the regime's economic program of nationalization and Arabization when he reaffirmed Algeria's need for French economic and cultural contribution.

Independent Algeria's Economy

Any sounding of Algeria's economic condition, eighteen months after independence, suffers from the lack of suitable depth, the absence of hard statistics, and the obvious fact that not much more than ultimate goals and means to achieve them can be surveyed. On one overwhelming question there is complete agreement: Algeria faced an extremely formidable economic problem. This was scarcely new on independence day but its complexity was multiplied by the war, and the necessary transition to be made when political control changed hands.

During the major portion of the first year, roughly half the Algerian population lacked employment. Life was kept going and mass starvation and disease were prevented by public and private aid from France and many other countries, including the United States. Algeria lacked enough trained cadres to cope with the maintenance of the underdeveloped machine the French had left. By 1964 fewer than 100,000 Europeans remained, but visiting experts, such as René Dumont, the renowned French agriculturist, performed remarkable work. France alone pumped perhaps $600,000,000 worth of various kinds of aid into Algeria. In all, approximately $1,000,000,000 aid reached the newly-independent country. Tax receipts accounted for no more than one-sixth of state expenditures. This state of affairs could not go on indefinitely, and the far more important question for long-range development depended mostly upon Algeria's efforts to help itself.

Aid was not expected, however, to dry up over night; and in 1964 France contributed roughly $200,000,000, while a credit from the Soviet Union of $100,000,000, repayable, with interest, in twelve years, has been accepted. Communist China extended an interest-free credit of $50,000,000. American aid, while not large, had an interesting format. A total of forty-two tons of surplus food were assigned to be used as part payment for wages for Algerian workers on four soil conservation and irrigation pilot projects. The food plus some thrifty experts and technicians, and tools, completed this American public contribution. Apart from the food, the cost totals around $1,000,000. Various other private American programs also operate in the new state.

Algeria's own posture to its economic problems involved a steady march along the planned economic road of socialism. At the outset, Algerians brought in the much needed 1962 harvest from the deserted European farms. Then European and some Algerian lands were nationalized. By 1964, the total nationalized acreage reached 6,500,000 acres, devoted mostly to cereals, the vine, and citrus orchards. Peasant management committees legally took over some 17,000 abandoned French farms in March 1963. The 1963 harvest proved to be amazingly abundant. The export of food, however, such as fresh vegetables and citrus fruit, depended largely upon the French consumer.

Industry in many sectors declined to one-third capacity. But in the Saharan oil enterprise this trend was reversed as production increased 25 per cent. The Evian accords set the rules for compensation to French owners whose property was nationalized, and in May 1963, the two countries agreed that one-fifth the French regular contribution, approximately $40,000,000, would be used to reimburse Europeans who had been nationalized for their costs in preparing the 1963 harvest.

For the first years, no tamperings with the Saharan oil statute took place, but oilmen on the spot believed nationalization would ultimately be the end result. France has warned against this and, for the moment, holds the whip hand since annual aid exceeds Algeria's share of oil royalties by roughly $150,000,000 per year. In 1963 Algeria obtained approximately $50,000,000 from these wells and production reached 25,000,000 tons. In addition the Saharan Organism, a Franco-Algerian administrative body set up by the Evian accords, expended another $20,000,000 on public works in the Sahara. The straitened circumstances of the Algerian government prevented the use of this income on development—$19,000,000 had to be diverted into the military budget.

Almost all elements in this Saharan picture could change rapidly. Algeria does have the right, under the Evian accords, to assign leases to anyone it chooses, for exploration of areas not already assigned. France, however, should get the preference if bids are the same. In late January 1964, an American syndicate which included Phillips, Tidewater, Sinclair, and Tenneco, a subsidiary of Tennessee Gas Transmission, were in Algiers negotiating with Ben Bella. There was some possibility that an Algerian National Company might be formed from this approach and that Algeria would hold 51 per cent control.

A great pipeline project, which would take the overload off the existing line from Hassi Messaoud to Bougie, by carrying oil from that field to Arzew, near Oran, is under financial consideration, and the Algerian state will surely be a part owner—an agreement with Kuwait provided Algeria a loan of $27,000,000 which should make this participation possible. Another Anglo-French-American project to bring natural gas from Hassi Rmel to Arzew, convert it into liquid methane, and transport it to Europe is far beyond preliminary planning. The plant, costing $64,000,000, should be completed in early 1964, and is one of the major foreign investments. The Algerian state demands a 20 per cent interest in this enterprise,, which is known as project "Camel" (*Compagnie Algérienne de Methane Liquide*). When operating, the plant will convert 1,500,000,000 cubic meters of gas per year. Envisaged in the future are pipelines running under the Mediterranean. Since known gas reserves in the Sahara amount to 1.5 trillion (1,500,000,000,000) cubic meters, the large investment and heavy transport costs seem justified, unless atomic energy should compete favorably for the large European market.

What is abundantly apparent from this quick probe into the embryonic economy of independent Algeria, is that the new state requires important supplies of capital to move forward. It is estimated that the agricultural program alone in the socialized sector needs $200,000,000 annual investment, the equal of France's total contribution. An investment code which guarantees against nationalization without just compensation and which accepts the principle of reasonable profit and the right to take profit out of the country, is on the statute books. The capitalist West tends, however, to shy away and dislikes socialization, or perhaps even more, instability. Imagine the embarrassing position of Bechir Boumaza, minister of economy, in New York and Washington in September 1963, sounding public and private investment sources when the "Kabylia revolt" and the Moroccan frontier skirmish broke out. If these winds were not enough to produce a storm, capitalists on Wall Street could ponder Ben Bella's promise to place "all the means of production between the hands of workers."

A socialist system requires a lot of planners and technicians and these, like capital, are in short supply. Most of the credits extended to Algeria, thus far, have been underspent as a result of inadequate planning, timidity, and sparse trained personnel. Enterprising risks so necessary to blaze the trail of productivity must be taken in either a socialist or capitalist system if stagnation is to be avoided. Such an élan must be encouraged by the FLN, but no party can produce trained experts in quantity at the drop of a hat. It is for this reason that Algeria welcomes the opportunity to send its young people abroad for training and gratefully receives experts who come to Algeria from the outside to work and counsel.[8] Given this need, it became a serious loss to Algeria (and the United States) when the Peace Corps found itself inadequately supplied of French-speaking corpsmen to respond to a suggestion put out from Algeria.

A program of austerity in the interest of accumulating investment capital has been adopted. Government officials could not expect to

[8] Much of the material incorporated in the previous paragraphs comes from *The New York Times*, "Economic Review of an Emerging Africa," January 20, 1964.

draw the same salaries their French equivalents once had. Cuts were ordered and accepted. Still, purchase of an embassy building in Paris for $1,720,000 or the spending of $1,000,000 to celebrate Independence Day in Algeria were scarcely consistent with austerity. The redeeming feature of this maturation process is, perhaps, that deputies like Mme Rabah Bitat stood up in the Assembly and pointed out these glaring inconsistencies. And Amar Ben Toumi, former minister of justice and member of the Khider faction, observed that the *comités de gestion* (self-management committees which took over farms and some small industry) actually "confided the management of an important resource to people who possessed no technical training." [9]

Time alone will tell the tale of Algerian economy under the independent regime. After eighteen months, what stand out are the extremely tough, unsolved problems. Yet such a serious and well-informed reporter as Jean-François Kahn, who spent considerable time and thought investigating the agrarian economy, noted that the "self-managed farms are doing more than surviving, they are living." Placing the socialist farms in proper perspective, he estimates no more than 100,000 agricultural workers and their families, out of a total peasant population of 7,000,000, whose active age group numbers 2,000,000, are thus far involved.

These farms face all kinds of difficulty as do private farmers. There is a great scarcity of administrative personnel; tractor and combine parts are rare; and the peasant mentality does not understand the marketing economics. The state tried to provide a pool of mechanics to service farm machines, but the pay ($160 per month) compared to that in the private sector ($240), was not attractive.

However, evaluation does take place among Algerian leaders and changes and adaptations have been made. Small businesses and plants have been returned to the private sector. Boumaza has underscored the need to correct the early plunge toward nationalization, and he has gone on record that no monetary devaluation will take place in the foreseeable future.[10]

Still the path of socialism, possibly in some form not yet found in the textbooks, has been selected, and unless the all-important FLN

[9] *Le Monde,* January 2, 1964.
[10] *Le Monde,* January 2, 1964.

alters the choice, which seems unlikely, this path will be followed. The serious question then becomes, can these people make this system yield the necessary minimum? Can the FLN pull out of the nation the amount of loyalty, devotion, and sacrifice which development imposes upon the first generation?

Anyone who has followed the Algerian Revolution during the last decade should have anticipated the passing of the old economic and social order. Particularly vulnerable, and surely expendable at the earliest moment—independence day—were those parts of the old which had sustained the colonial interests. In the "distant" past, in 1958, Pierre Bourdieu, the intuitive French sociologist-anthropologist predicted,

> A society which has been so greatly revolutionized demands that revolutionary solutions be devised to meet its problems. It will insist that a way be found to mobilize these masses who have been freed from the traditional disciplines and thrown into a chaotic, disillusioned world, by holding up before them a collective ideal, the building of a harmonious social order and the development of a modern economy capable of assuring employment and a decent standard of living for all.[11]

THE MAGHRIB IN THE MODERN WORLD

All over independent North Africa, rapid changes are taking place in the traditions of Arabo-Berber society. Islam yields to modern needs, but it does so unevenly, preserving some traditions and casting off others. Change is greater in the urban and coastal zone, but, as we have seen, it reaches into the back country in Tunisia and Algeria where older agricultural methods and social structures change, too. Within the new generation which attends school, and particularly those young people who receive advanced education, often outside their native land, the urge to reform is very great.

Tunisia and Algeria, and Morocco to a lesser degree, altered the status of women, thus revolutionizing the life of half the inhabitants. Sometimes it takes a long time for practice and custom to take cog-

[11] Originally published as *Sociologie de l'Algérie* (Paris: Presses Universitaires de France, 1958), reissued as *The Algerians* (Boston: Beacon Press, 1962) in English translation by Alan C. M. Ross, from which this quotation is taken, pp. 191-92.

nizance of the law, as we ourselves can see all over the United States today. In Algeria, the participation of young women in the revolution was, by itself, an enormous change in behavior. Girls, who had never been on the streets without their mothers or chaperons, journeyed many miles alone, carrying messages (or grenades and weapons) concealed under their flowing dress. Married Muslim women whose husbands and sons were in the field with the FLN took unknown freedom fighters who needed refuge into their homes. The chorus of tongue clicking among the grandfathers failed to impede these women who entered the male world.

No one can predict the rate of this change which is taking place in the traditional North African society, but it will surely move the people toward the modern world. Islam and long standing Arabo-Berber civilization will not disappear; they will modify. Arabic and Islam are built-in characteristcis destined to be around for a very long time. The withdrawal of France can best be psychologically expressed by a return, perhaps an exaggerated one, to the sheltering arms of Islam. But since independence, many more students and government missions reach out not simply to Europe but to the world.

What kind of a posture do these states present in international relations? Imagine a series of concentric circles as one finds in an archery target. At the center, where it counts most, the North African states asserted their independence. They fought hard for it, desperately hard in Algeria's case, and they are not about to alienate it. On the contrary, they are consolidating it. Tunisia is pleased to see France evacuate Bizerte, even though six thousand Tunisians who worked in the complex must seek new jobs. Morocco feels the same about the evacuation of the American bases, scheduled for 1964. Algeria, in the Evian accords, agreed to respect various French military, naval, and air installations on its soil. The air-naval base at Mers-El-Kébir, for example, is leased to France for fifteen years. French atomic technical facilities at Reggane are to be kept for five years. The new state will surely press France for a change on these agreements; and already it protests French atomic explosions.

Going from the center toward the outer circle of the target, there is the relationship between these three Maghribi states themselves. Unity, federation, or confederation are concepts upon which millions of words have been written and spoken. There are strong foundations for the concept, though almost no historical precedent. Cultural unity is already a fact in the broad sense. The economies have a common base, and all three states, whether they like it or not, have long standing cultural and economic ties with France. But when it comes right down to political unification, impelling forces and recent political action deny this.

Morocco is a kingdom, Tunisia a presidential republic, Algeria a popular socialist republic. A unitary state could not possibly accommodate either the three leaders or the political structures of each. Cooperation at some levels at various times of mutual interest is the best expectation. And there have been times of lack of cooperation, as in Bourguiba's plunge toward Marker 233 in July 1961, and the recent fighting on the Algerian-Moroccan frontier. Tunisia's sponsorship of independent Mauretania led to the recall of the Moroccan ambassador and much recrimination. As in the best regulated families, there is unity and diversity, cooperation and jealousy, love and hate. Only at the level of the most "progressive" political element, the socialist activists of the cities with their peasant supporters, can there be found an authentic basic unity, *une Révolution de base*. The Algerians speak of it most often, for their government and party embodies this viewpoint. Militant minorities in Tunisia and Morocco also think along these lines, but this does not imply that future socialist governments would unify the Maghrib.

At the still larger circle of the "Arab nation," stretching from Baghdad to Casablanca, unity in political terms becomes still more abstract. These recently independent North African states are jealous of their freedom, and, while they pay oral tribute to Arab unity and belong to the Arab League, their acts relate directly to national interest. The FLN appreciated Cairo's support in the revolution, yet its headquarters were removed to Tunis before the struggle ended. Since independence, there is no concrete evidence of any intimate political consolidation. Bourguiba expelled Nasser's representatives from Tunisia, yet after the Bizerte fiasco in July 1961, he drew closer to this Arab brother. Morocco arrested Egyptian officers who served with Algerian forces, fighting in the disputed western Sahara in Ocober 1963, and some harsh exchanges passed between Rabat and Cairo. Arab disunity can be quickly transformed in special cases, as when Israel planned to divert the Jordan River. The Maghribi states, however, have never regarded Israel with the same militancy as the eastern Arabs, and they showed no interest in joining actively the entangled web of middle Eastern politics.

More vague is the circle, of recent origin, which relates to African unity. Though contacts between the peoples of the Maghrib and those of sub-Saharan Africa have existed for centuries, these were essentially commercial and between individuals or tribes. With the coming of independence, the new states exchanged officials, teachers, and trade economists. Phrases like "Pan Africanism" and "African Unity" began to be heard.

The independent Maghrib records in its constitutions, and in the press, its connection with Africa. There have been a multitude of conferences and much visitation back and forth. Then, it is interesting to note that Islam is the fastest spreading religion in Africa. Bourguiba traveled to Accra to celebrate Ghana's independence (1957). The following year at the Accra Conference, Morocco and Tunisia joined six additional African countries and participated in resolutions favoring Algerian independence. Later that year, Guinea voted its way out of the French Union and Sekou Touré strongly endorsed and supported, as best he could, the Algerian cause. Tunis played host to the African People's Congress in 1960, the year in which sixteen African states obtained independence.

The Congo question brought Moroccan and Tunisian soldiers into that land, and also FLN observers. The United Arab Republic and the FLN backed Lumumba; Tunisia supported the UN position. The FLN viewed Lumumba as the authentic leader of the people and admired his resistance to "neo-colonialism"; various French officers who had fought the FLN and later deserted, to serve Moise Tschombe in Katanga, helped the FLN make its decision. The FLN newspaper, *El Moudjahid*, of September 23, 1961, claimed that Kasavubu and Mobutu received 56,000,000 francs for turning Lumumba over to his assassins. A "Casablanca Group," Morocco, UAR, Guinea, Ghana, Mali, plus observers from Libya and the FLN, took shape in 1961 and created a council and committees (economic, military, cultural).

Finally, in the summer of 1963, the Organization of African Unity set itself up at Addis Ababa.

What these organizations and Africanism, the underlying spirit, will have in common for the long run is hard to say. All independent African states endorse the same evolution for the remaining colonies. Algeria, for example, helps equip and train Angolese freedom fighters. No African state wishes a resurgence of colonial penetration or "neo-colonialism"; a kind of African Monroe Doctrine has thus taken shape. All these states face problems of development. Thus far, cultural exchange, trade missions, mediation between skirmishing African states seem to be the major functions of these various organizations.

All Africa must ponder its relationship with the European common market. Some states benefit from affiliation with the EEC; others have their own customs union. Still others, like Algeria, have yet to decide whether to apply for association with EEC. Possibly Africanism and its resultant structures will evolve somewhat like Latin-Americanism and serve to unify action in some matters, and as a discussion platform for other truly difficult problems. Certainly Pan-Africanism, like Latin-Americanism, represents a posture generally critical of old attitudes stemming from Western dominion. In some respects, Africa is becoming a self-appointed Western conscience. It seeks to relieve the East-West cold war pattern of too much "hard line."

In the United Nations, where our circle opens up to world-sized radius, the Maghribi states usually can be found in the Afro-Asian bloc on most questions. But there are cases, such as that of Mauretania's admission, where sparks crackled between Morocco and Tunisia—thus far, Algeria ignores Mauretania, either out of respect for Morocco or from considerations of future bargaining power with that state in the frontier dispute.

All these states open their doors to the United States, the Soviet Union, and the Chinese People's Republic. In 1963 Bourguiba promised to support Communist China's entry into the UN, as de Gaulle intends, since he, too, has recognized that state (to the keen disappointment of Washington). Tunisia, Morocco, and Algeria will also accept aid from all three blocs, so long as the strings do not strangle.

Probably Tunisia is the most American oriented and Morocco the most Gaullist.

Algeria's FLN constantly pleaded with the United States during the revolution, though obviously there were no official contacts, to stop the flow of NATO arms into the hands of French soldiers. Since independence, Algerian relations with the United States have been correct if not enthusiastic on both sides. States like these three realize that their evolution resembles more closely the underdeveloped world, including Soviet Russia and Communist China, than the United States and Western Europe. For this reason, there exists a zone of sympathy and rapport lacking with the West. Yet it is equally clear that France, Western Europe, and the United States are in a position to direct more financial and technical support to North Africa. In this, France is far and away the leader, despite all the opprobrium of the colonial past.

Morocco had its heroic and respected king; Tunisia its tightly-knit Neo-Destour and able and conciliatory leaders; Algeria its revolution with the attending martyrs and heroes, and its rapid social change. In these countries, the people now have the responsibility of their future development. The West's responsibility lays perhaps in the fact that these countries were not sufficiently prepared for nationhood. But, from here on, their destiny becomes their own, and whatever may happen in the years ahead, they have what they most wanted—independence. They are no longer colonials but Moroccans, Tunisians, and Algerians, struggling like the rest of us to survive and grow in a complex and shrinking world.

An exceedingly large literature relating to the Maghrib exists in the French language, and in recent years the output in English has increased. It should not be forgotten that many primary documents are to be found in various official French collections, and since independence documents are piling up in Rabat, Tunis, and Algiers. The archives of the Makhzan, while not generally accessible, help greatly to explain Morocco's history from the inside instead of from the colonial surface exterior. In recent years, books written by Moroccan, Tunisian, and Algerian authors have begun to appear.

Benjamin Rivlin's "A Selective Survey of the Literature in the Social Sciences and Related Fields on Modern North Africa," *The American Political Science Review*, 48 (Sept. 1954), 826-848, is a good survey of work through 1952. Much more comprehensive is Roger Le Tourneau, M. Flory, and J.-P. Trystram, "L'Afrique du Nord: état des travaux," *Revue Française de Science Politique*, 9 (June 1959), pp. 410-453, which examines the output of books and articles. Many of the books mentioned later contain critical bibliographies.

Almost the only recent survey in English of the history of the Maghrib as a whole, is that edited by Nevill Barbour, A *Survey of Northwest Africa* (*the Maghrib*) (London, 1959). This monopoly has been somewhat broken by Charles Gallagher's *The United States and North Africa* (Cambridge, Mass., 1963), a thoughtful book with much on North Africa and little on the United States or American relations with North Africa. Charles-André Julien, the impressive French scholar, provides *L'Histoire de l'Afrique du Nord* (*Tunisie, Algérie, Maroc*), 2 vols., (Paris, 1931), revised by Charles Courtois and Roger Le Tourneau in 1952-1953; his sensitive and highly competent *L'Afrique du Nord en Marche, nationalismes musulmans et souveraineté française* (Paris, 1952); his work on the Algerian revolution is momentarily expected. The process of nationalism has been thoroughly investigated and vigorously written up by Lorna Hahn, *North Africa: Nationalism to Nationhood* (Washington, 1960). The French administrator, school official, and scholar Roger Le Tourneau presents a more or less official French account in his *Evolution politique de l'Afrique du Nord musulmane, 1920-1961* (Paris, 1962). Carleton Coon's *Caravan: the Story of the Middle East* (New York, 1958) and Pierre Bourdieu's *The Algerians* (Boston, 1961) provide the reader with the insights of the anthropologist and sociologist, respectively. Ethnographical and economic questions, as well as demographic matters, are beautifully discussed in Jean Despois, *L'Afrique du Nord* (Paris, 1949).

The same author produced two books of merit on Tunisian geography, *La Tunisie: Ses régions* (Paris, 1961) and the regional study, *La Tunisie orientale: Sahel et Basse steppe* (Paris, 2nd ed., 1955). Of a political orientation are the works of Jean Rous, *Tunisie . . . Attention!* (Paris, 1952), Habib Bourguiba, *La Tunisie et la France* (Paris, 1954) and his *Propos et entretiens* (Tunis, 1960), mostly articles and interviews given by the Neo-Destour leader. Henry de Montéty, *Les femmes de Tunisie* (Paris, 1958) touches a vital issue, and André Raymond's *La Tunisie* (Paris, 1961) in the *Que sais-je?* series is extremely useful. A fine survey is Henri Terrasse, *Histoire de Maroc des origines à l'établissement du protectorat français*, 2 vols. (Casablanca, 1949-1950). Hilary Tee made an English translation in 1952.

Morocco has attracted many scholars in recent years. Rom Landau's *Moroccan Drama, 1900-1955* (London, 1956) is a sympathetic account by an old hand. Douglas Ashford, in his *Political Change in Morocco* (Princeton, 1961), intensively surveys in Ph.D. thesis style political forces between 1955 and 1959. Important studies of an earlier period are Robert Montagne, *Les Berbères et le Makhzen dans le Sud du Maroc* (Paris, 1930), a study in political sociology and his survey of Moroccan urban society, *Naissance du prolétariat marocain: enquête collective executée de 1948 à 1950* (Paris, 1952). Marshal Louis Lyautey left several literary monuments: *Paroles d'action* (Paris, 1927) and *Textes et Lettres* (1912-1925) 4 vols., ed. by Pierre Lyautey (Paris, 1953-1957). General Georges Catroux's biography, *Lyautey le Marocain* (Paris, 1952) does full justice to France's greatest colonial administrator. Of more recent orientation is Robert Rezette, *Les partis politiques marocaines* (Paris, 1955), a storehouse of precise data. Gilbert Grandval in *Ma Mission au Maroc* (Paris, 1956) tells the sad story with considerable sympathy and insight. Books like Jacques Berque's *Structures sociales du Haut Atlas* (Paris, 1955) provide deep insights into rural society while Roger Le Tourneau, in his *Fès avant le Protectorat* (Casablanca, 1949), a French doctorat *ès lettres* thesis, probes deeply into traditional urban Muslim society. Jean and Simone Lacouture examine recent history in high class journalistic fashion in *Le Maroc à l'epreuve* (Paris, 1958). Rom Landau's *Morocco Independent* (New York, 1961) and his *The Moroccans Yesterday and Today* (London, 1963) are extremely useful to the reader seeking to judge current developments. Graham H. Stuart, *The International City of Tangier* (Stanford, 1953) exhausts the subject. Finally, Allal al-Fassi's *Independence Movements in North Africa* (Washington, 1954) is a strong statement by Istiqlal's leader.

An overwhelming number of books on the Algerian revolution and its immediate background have appeared. In 1962, in Tunis, at the *Centre de Documentation* of the GPRA, located at 23 Avenue Bab Djedid, some four hundred such books lined the shelves. Nor is the literature on the pre 1954 period slender. The problem, therefore, is one of selection. Augustin Bernard's *L'Algérie* (Paris, 1930) is a straight general, and fairly official, history published a century after the conquest of Algiers. Today's Algerian counterpart is André Nouschi, Yves Lacoste, and André Prenant, *L'Algérie passé et present* (Paris, 1960) "solidly documented" and slanted toward the Marxist nationalist line. André Nouschi's doctoral dissertation, *Enquête sur le niveau de vie des populations rurales constantinoises de la conquête jusqu'en 1919, essai d'histoire économique et sociale* (Paris, 1961), inspired by and dedicated to Marc Bloc, is one of the finest contributions to the literature in the last half-century. A large number of French scholars contributed to *Initiation à l'Algérie* (Paris, 1957), basically a French official account—there are also similar books for Morocco and Tunisia. Two other useful works are, Jacques Lambert, *Manuel de la législation algérienne* (Algiers, 1952) and René Gendarme, *L'Économie algérienne* (Paris, 1959), which digests the Maspétiol and Delavignette reports.

No other recent revolution has stimulated such a distinguished list of literary talent. Albert Camus, in his *Actuelles III, Chroniques algériennes, 1939-1958* (Paris, 1958) dealt sensitively with misery in the Kabylia, in 1939, and projected his thought to the state of war in 1958. Born in Algeria, Camus was nearly lynched when he returned there in 1936 and told the colons the facts of life in the outer world. After Camus died, his friend Jules Roy produced *La guerre d'Algérie* (Paris, 1960), in English translation, *The War in Algeria* (New York, 1961), a first-class indictment of the thinking of the French military by a former colonel who, miraculously, knew how to write. The next year Roy wrote *Autour du drame* (Paris, 1961), which ended on a cease-fire plea, "Il faut que cette guerre s'arrête." Jean-Paul Sartre wrote many articles against the official French position and delivered innumerable lectures, and Simone de Beauvoir, with the help of Gisèle Halimi, put together *Djamila Boupacha* (Paris, 1962) from various documents to show how the French forces tortured an Algerian girl and how French "justice" supported the army until finally the case reached a fair-minded and brave judge in Caen. Picasso donated the illustrations.

During the course of the Algerian revolution Germaine Tillion, the French ethnographer of the Maghrib at the Sorbonne, wrote two books, *Algeria: the Realities*, translated by Ronald Mathews (New York, 1958) and *France and Algeria, Complementary Enemies*, translated by Richard Howard (New York, 1961). Mme Tillion's ethnography was excellent, but her early political judgment missed the target by a wide mark—until 1956 she thought Algeria would remain French. One of the better accounts of the revolution was Charles-Henri Favrod's *La Révolution algérienne* (Paris, 1959) which contained many basic documents. This Swiss journalist up-dated his work in *Le FLN et l'Algérie* (Paris, 1962). In English Michael Clark, who reported the early years of revolution for *The New York Times* wrote *Algeria in Turmoil* (New York, 1959), in which he supported French Algeria. Joan Gillespie's *Algeria: Rebellion and Revolution* (New York, 1961) emphasized the dynamics of the FLN, and Richard and Joan Brace in *Ordeal in Algeria* (New York, 1960) related Algeria to the French political crisis and concluded that Algeria would gain independence. Joseph Kraft, a speech-writer for the late President Kennedy and a journalist, in his *Struggle for Algeria* (New York, 1961) reached the conclusion that independence was at hand and the FLN would dominate the country. Edward Behr's *The Algerian Problem* (London, 1961) reached the same answers and hoped that cultural, economic, and social ties would be preserved between France and Algeria. The cultural question was explored by David Gordon in *North Africa's French Legacy, 1954-1962* (Cambridge, Mass., 1962).

Insight into the ideology of the FLN can best be found in the works of Franz Fanon, a West Indian psychiatrist who joined the Algerian cause. His earliest book *Peau Noire, Masques Blancs* (Paris, 1952) examines the psychology of racialism. *L'an V de la Révolution algérienne* (Paris, 1960) is an analysis of Algerian voices, the family, medicine, and colonialism, and the European minority. Finally, *Les damnés de la terre* (Paris, 1961) goes into the questions of violence, national grandeur, and colonial warfare's mental troubles. More than any author Fanon seemed to be in touch with the feelings and aspirations of the Algerians.

INDEX